Best Easy Day Hikes
Syracuse

Help Us Keep This Guide Up to Date

Every effort has been made by the author and editors to make this guide as accurate and useful as possible. However, many things can change after a guide is published—regulations change, facilities come under new management, and so forth.

We would love to hear from you concerning your experiences with this guide and how you feel it could be improved and kept up to date. While we may not be able to respond to all comments and suggestions, we'll take them to heart, and we'll also make certain to share them with the author. Please send your comments and suggestions to falconeditorial@rowman .com.

Thanks for your input!

Best Easy Day Hikes Series

Best Easy Day Hikes
Syracuse

Second Edition

Randi Minetor

FALCONGUIDES

ESSEX, CONNECTICUT

FALCONGUIDES®

An imprint of Globe Pequot, the trade division of The Rowman & Littlefield Publishing Group, Inc.
4501 Forbes Blvd., Ste. 200
Lanham, MD 20706
www.rowman.com

Falcon and FalconGuides are registered trademarks and Make Adventure Your Story is a trademark of The Rowman & Littlefield Publishing Group, Inc.

Distributed by NATIONAL BOOK NETWORK

Cover Photo by Nic Minetor

Maps by The Rowman & Littlefield Publishing Group, Inc.

British Library Cataloguing-in-Publication Information available

Library of Congress Cataloging-in-Publication Data

ISBN 978-1-4930-7594-2 (paper: alk. paper)
ISBN 978-1-4930-7595-9 (electronic)

♾️™ The paper used in this publication meets the minimum requirements of American National Standard for Information Sciences—Permanence of Paper for Printed Library Materials, ANSI/NISO Z39.48-1992.

The author and The Rowman & Littlefield Publishing Group, Inc. assume no liability for accidents happening to, or injuries sustained by, readers who engage in the activities described in this book.

Contents

Acknowledgments

First and foremost, I am so grateful to my husband, Nic Minetor, for walking nearly all these trails with me, keeping me from getting hopelessly lost in the woods, and knowing far better than I when it was time to stop hiking, stop writing, and see our friends again.

Thanks to everyone on the team at FalconGuides; they do such a careful and beautiful job in bringing our books to fruition. To my brilliant agent, Regina Ryan, I am undyingly grateful for all she does to manage the business of publishing on my behalf.

I have so many friends to whom I am grateful, but Ken Horowitz and Rose-Anne Moore, Martha and Peter Schermerhorn, Kristen Kessler, and Cindy Blair stand out from this group for their unflagging encouragement and support. For the first edition of this book, my lifelong friend Martin Winer helped keep up the pace, especially on a three-trail day that will live in infamy.

Introduction

It's moments before dawn at the edge of a forested wetland surrounded by river and canal, as several small groups of people with binoculars in hand stand stock-still, listening intently.

There it is—the distant "Who cooks for you?" call of a barred owl, one of more than one hundred species that nest and breed in the refuge's forests. As darkness begins to recede and the light turns dawn-gray, a chirrup in the reeds on the edge of the forest signals a marsh wren's presence. A "witchity, witchity, witchity" song reveals a common yellow-throat's location, while deeper in the woods, combinations of lyrical notes and lisping buzzes tell birders that black-throated green and black-throated blue warblers have arrived overnight.

With the brightening sky, more snatches of song fill the air. A rabbit crosses the now-visible path onto the island, and chipmunks begin their familiar sharp "chit" notes.

Where is this magical place? It's a few miles west of Syracuse at Howland Island, in the Northern Montezuma Wetlands Complex—one of many such refuges, forests, and preserves that provide homes to all manner of wildlife. Trails through this and more than a dozen other preserves present some of the most satisfying, easy hiking in the central New York region—all in places that allow us to connect with our natural world and all within an hour's drive of downtown Syracuse.

Take the Cliff Trail at Clark Reservation State Park or gaze beyond the cascading water at Chittenango Falls and see limestone and sandstone born as much as 400 million years ago, when a shallow sea covered much of North America.

Clark Reservation's cliff edges rise high over the valley below, but they were not always so lofty. A diligently flowing creek created these tall places, wearing away at the stone banks until they became walls as the creek sank lower. Today we enjoy wide vistas and impressive rock formations because of millions of years of geology at work.

While limestone forms the bedrock of central New York, much of the landscape shows the effects of more-current events. Walk the ridgeline on the Esker Brook Trails in the Montezuma National Wildlife Refuge, circle the deep turquoise pools at Green Lakes State Park, or stroll the boardwalk to the kettle pond at Labrador Hollow Unique Area and see the impact of glaciers that moved over this land as recently as 20,000 years ago.

We know that receding glaciers hollowed out the crevasses that would become the Finger Lakes, but we may forget that the unusually deep ponds and small lakes are the products of huge blocks of ice that fell from calving glaciers, creating holes in the earth. When the ice blocks melted, they filled these holes with water, and lakes were born. Today we can circle these unusual bodies of water on easy, level trails that reveal the lakes' unusual character.

There's at least one more chapter of natural history to discover in the Syracuse area: the twentieth century reforestation that's still in progress. We can enjoy easy or more rugged hikes through Huckleberry Swamp, Baltimore Woods, Bear Swamp State Forest, and High Vista Preserve because of the combined work of man and nature to reclaim this land. Not so long ago—as recently as the 1930s—these properties were farmers' fields, used to graze cattle or grow crops. Today they are covered with young forests, planted in part by the legendary Civilian Conservation Corps of the Great Depression era. A delightful wilderness experience awaits visitors who explore each area on well-marked and maintained trails.

Intermixed with these excellent hiking experiences are some crown jewels just beyond Syracuse. Highland Forest County Park, with its meticulously labeled trails that traverse truly beautiful surroundings, offers one of the finest days out we've found anywhere. Fillmore Glen, the southernmost park in this guide, pairs an adventurous hike—aided by eight unobtrusive bridges—with a spectacular gorge, waterfalls, and startlingly emerald foliage.

Beaver Lake Nature Center, just north of the city in Baldwinsville, offers a series of delightful trails featuring an extended boardwalk along a tranquil lake. To the west, trails through Seneca Meadows Wetland Preserve wind between ponds where American and least bitterns and pied-billed grebes raise their young. And the shores of Lake Ontario offer one of the area's most remarkable formations—Chimney Bluffs, where wind and weather combine to influence a towering, ever-changing coastline.

With so many options for day hikes, residents and visitors alike will find plenty of outdoor adventures that showcase the best of central New York—and all less than an hour's drive from the city of Syracuse.

Weather

Few places can match central New York for its gorgeous spring and summer, when flowers scent the air, leaves fairly burst from the trees in intense shades of green, and the sky turns cobalt to complement the sunlight.

The sun shines six days out of ten from June through August. Spring temperatures can linger in the 50s and 60s until June; idyllic summer days can average in the 70s and

80s, with occasional spikes into the 90s in June or July and cooler temperatures at night. Heavy rains often arrive in April, although they rarely last more than a day or two at a time. Syracuse has no dry season, so be prepared for rain any time you visit.

To truly appreciate this transformation to the Technicolor spring and summer seasons in upstate New York, however, we must face the Syracuse area's legendary winters. The city once rated fourth among the top-ten snowiest cities in America, and its heavy snowfalls continue to make national news.

Winter temperatures average in the mid-20s, with significant dips into the 20s, 10s, and single digits in January, February, and March. Check the windchill factor before making a winter hike, as the air can feel much colder than the temperature indicates. The annual February thaw can push temperatures into the 50s for a few days, but the cold will return, usually lasting into mid-April. Snow is guaranteed—an average winter sees 115 inches (that's 9.5 feet), although not all at once. In the winter months, November through January, the Syracuse area sees the sun about 28 percent of the time.

Fall equals spring in its spectacle, with days in the 50s and 60s, bright blue skies, and foliage panoramas throughout the area's parks and preserves.

Park and Preserve Regulations

You will find the lands listed in this book both accessible and fairly easy to navigate. Only the state parks listed charge admission fees (though some preserves suggest a donation).

While some of the parks have picnic areas with trash receptacles, most of the parks, forests, and preserves are "carry-in, carry-out" areas. This means you must take all your trash with you for disposal outside the park. Glass containers are not permitted in any of the parks.

Some preserves do not permit pets, and in all cases where they are allowed, dogs and other pets must be leashed. You will see dogs running free in some parks, but park regulations and county leash laws prohibit this. It's also illegal to leave your dog's droppings in the park; you can face fines for not cleaning up after your pet.

If you're a gun owner, you will need to leave your weapon at home when entering a county park, as only law enforcement officers are permitted to carry guns on these lands. Hunting is permitted in properties managed by the Department of Environmental Conservation, so it's a good idea to wear a blaze orange jacket and hat if you're planning to hike these areas during hunting seasons.

Safety and Preparation

There is little to fear when hiking in upstate New York, whether you're stepping down into the gorge at Fillmore Glen or hiking through Bear Swamp State Forest. Some basic safety precautions and intelligent preparation will make your hikes calamity-free.

- **Wear proper footwear.** A pair of good, correctly fitting hiking shoes or boots can make all the difference on a daylong hike, or even on a short walk. Look for socks that wick away moisture, or add sock liners to your footwear system.

- **Carry a first-aid kit** to deal with blisters, cuts and scrapes, and insect bites and stings. Insects abound in late spring and summer in central New York, especially near wetlands, ponds, lakes, and creeks, so wear insect repellent and carry after-bite ointment or cream to apply to itchy spots.

- **Protect against ticks.** Deer ticks that carry Lyme disease, babesiosis, and other chronic illnesses are rampant in New York State. Your best defense is your clothing—long sleeves, long pants, and socks—but barring this, choose an insect repellent with permethrin, the most effective tick killer, and check your body for ticks when you leave the trail. If you do find a tick, don't panic—it takes up to 36 hours for the tick to transfer a disease to your bloodstream. Remove the tick with tweezers, being careful not to squeeze the body as you do so. Watch for a rash or other redness to develop, especially a "bull's-eye" rash with a big red ring around the bite site, which indicates Lyme disease; flu-like symptoms also may mean Lyme or another tick-borne illness. Call your doctor if any of these symptoms appear.

- **Carry water.** Don't try drinking from the rivers, creeks, ponds, or other bodies of water unless you can filter or treat the water first. Your best bet is to carry your own—at least a quart per person for any hike and up to a gallon in hot weather.

- **Dress in layers,** no matter what the season. If you're a vigorous hiker, you'll want to peel off a layer or two even in the dead of winter. On a summer evening, the air can cool suddenly after sunset, and rain clouds can erupt with little preamble.

- **Bring your mobile phone.** All the trails in this book have mobile coverage, so if you do get into a jam, help is a phone call away. (As a courtesy to the rest of us, set your phone to vibrate while you're on the trail.)

- **Leave wildlife alone.** Central New York State once was home to the timber rattlesnake, but scientists believe this species to be extirpated from the areas covered in this book. Black bear sightings are very rare. As a general rule, don't approach wildlife of any kind. If you do see a bear, don't get any closer; if your presence changes its behavior, you're too close. Keep your distance and the bear will most likely do the same. Some cases of rabies in raccoons have been reported in the area; generally it's best to steer clear of these animals when they're seen in daylight.

Zero Impact

Many trails in the Syracuse area are heavily used year-round. As trail users and advocates, we must be especially vigilant to make sure our passage leaves no lasting mark. Here are some basic guidelines for preserving trails in the region.

- **Pack out all your own trash,** including biodegradable items such as orange peels. You might also pack out garbage left by less considerate hikers.
- **Don't approach or feed any wild creatures**—the gray squirrel eyeing your snack food is best able to survive if it remains self-reliant. Feeding ducks and geese can spread illnesses among the birds when they come into contact while chasing bits of bread or corn. Please don't feed them.
- **Don't pick wildflowers** or gather rocks, antlers, feathers, and other treasures along the trail. Removing these items will only take away from the next hiker's experience.

- **Avoid damaging trailside soils and plants** by remaining on the established route. This is also a good rule of thumb for avoiding poison ivy and poison sumac, common regional trailside irritants.
- **Be courteous** by not making loud noises while hiking.
- **Many of these trails are multiuse,** which means you'll share them with other hikers, trail runners, cyclists, and horseback riders. Familiarize yourself with the proper trail etiquette, yielding the trail when appropriate.
- **Use restrooms or outhouses** at trailheads or along the trail.

Land Management Agencies

These government and non-profit organizations manage most of the public lands described in this guide. They can provide further information on these hikes and other trails in the greater Syracuse area.

- Montezuma National Wildlife Refuge, 3395 US 20, Seneca Falls, NY 13148; (315) 568-5987; www.fws.gov/refuge/montezuma
- New York State Department of Environmental Conservation, Region 7 Office, 615 Erie Blvd. West, Syracuse, NY 13204; (315) 426-7400; www.dec.ny.gov
- Onondaga County Parks & Recreation, 106 Lake Dr., Liverpool NY 13088; (315) 451-7275; onondagacounty parks.com
- New York State Office of Parks, Recreation and Historic Preservation, 625 Broadway, Albany, NY 12207; (518) 474-0456; https://parks.ny.gov
- Seneca Meadows Inc., 1786 Salcman Rd., Waterloo, NY 13165; (315) 539-5624; senecameadows.com

How to Use This Guide

This guide is designed to be simple and easy to use. Each hike is described with a map and summary information that delivers the trail's vital statistics, including length, difficulty, fees and permits, park hours, canine compatibility, and trail contacts. Directions to the trailhead are also provided, along with a general description of what you'll see along the way. A detailed route finder (Miles and Directions) sets forth mileages between significant landmarks along the trail.

Hike Selection

This guide describes trails accessible to every hiker, whether they are visiting from out of town or living in the greater Syracuse area. The hikes are no longer than 8 miles round-trip, and some are considerably shorter. They range in difficulty from flat excursions perfect for a family outing to more challenging treks along the area's gorges and ravines. While these trails are among the best, keep in mind that nearby trails, often in the same park or preserve, may offer options better suited to your needs.

I've sought to space hikes throughout the Onondaga, Cayuga, Madison, Cortland, and Wayne County areas. Wherever your starting point, you'll find a great easy day hike nearby.

Difficulty Ratings

These are all easy hikes, but easy is a relative term. Some would argue that no hike involving any kind of climbing is easy, but in the Syracuse area, hills and ravines are a fact of life. To aid in the selection of a hike that suits particular needs and abilities, each is rated easy, moderate, or more challenging. Bear in mind that even more challenging routes can be made easy by hiking within your limits and taking rests when you need them.

- **Easy** hikes are generally short and flat, taking no longer than 1 hour to complete.
- **Moderate** hikes involve increased distance and relatively mild changes in elevation; they will take 1 to 2 hours to complete.
- **More challenging** hikes feature some steep stretches and/or greater distances; they generally will take longer than 2 hours to complete.

These are completely subjective ratings—consider that what you think is easy is entirely dependent on your level of fitness and the adequacy of your gear (primarily shoes). If you are hiking with a group, you should select a hike with a rating that's appropriate for the least fit and prepared in your party.

Approximate hiking times are based on the assumption that on flat ground most walkers average 2 miles per hour. Adjust that rate by the steepness of the terrain and your level of fitness (subtract time if you're an aerobic animal; add time if you're hiking with kids) and you have a ballpark hiking duration. Be sure to add more time if you plan to picnic or take part in other activities such as bird watching or photography.

Trail Finder

Best Hikes for Birders

1   Beaver Lake Nature Center: Lake Loop Trail

7   Montezuma National Wildlife Refuge:
South Spring Pool and Esker Brook Trails

8   Montezuma National Wildlife Refuge: Seneca Trail

9   Northern Montezuma WMA: Howland Island

10   Seneca Meadows Wetland Preserve

12   Huckleberry Swamp

14   Labrador Hollow State Unique Area

15   Highland Forest County Park

17   High Vista Preserve

Best Hikes for Waterfalls

3   Pratt's Falls Park

5   Chittenango Falls State Park

18   Fillmore Glen State Park

Best Hikes for Water Views

1   Beaver Lake Nature Center: Lake Loop Trail

2   Clark Reservation State Park

4   Green Lakes State Park

8   Montezuma NWR: Seneca Trail

9   Northern Montezuma WMA: Howland Island

13   Chimney Bluffs State Park

14   Labrador Hollow State Unique Area

Best Hikes for Fall Foliage

Best Hikes for Panoramic Views

Map Legend

Symbol	Description
═══81═══	Interstate Highway
──20──	U.S. Highway
═══370═══	State Highway
──80──	Local Road
= = = = =	Unpaved Road
▬▬▬▬▬	Featured Trail
- - - - - -	Trail
～～～	River/Creek
⬭	Body of Water
‖‖‖‖‖‖	Boardwalk/Steps
‿	Bridge
▲	Camping
❷	Information Center
🅿	Parking
⌖	Picnic Area
■	Point of Interest/Structure
🚻	Restroom
○	Town
❶	Trailhead
❀	Viewpoint/Overlook

1 Beaver Lake Nature Center: Lake Loop Trail

Wander the perimeter of Beaver Lake through meadows, woods, and bog for a generous sampling of all the earthly delights this nature center offers.

Distance: 3.0-mile loop

Approximate hiking time: 1.25 hours

Difficulty: Easy

Trail surface: Packed dirt trail and boardwalk

Best season: Apr through Nov

Other trail users: Joggers, cross-country skiers

Canine compatibility: Dogs not permitted

Fees and permits: Entrance fee per vehicle, paid as you exit; annual pass available

Schedule: Open daily, 7:30 a.m. to 7:30 p.m. (open at 7 a.m. on Monday from first Monday in May to Labor Day); closed Thanksgiving and Christmas

Maps: Onondaga County Parks; onondagacountyparks.com /assets/Uploads/Beaver-Lake -Nature-Center/BLNCTrail-Map.jpg

Water availability: At the visitor center

Trail contact: Beaver Lake Nature Center, 8477 East Mud Lake Rd., Baldwinsville 13027; (315) 638-2519; https://onon-dagacountyparks.com/parks/ beaver-lake-nature-center

Finding the trailhead: From Syracuse on I-690 North, exit at West Genesee Street (NY 370). Turn west (left) and drive 1.8 miles to East Mud Lake Road. Turn right onto East Mud Lake and continue to the nature center entrance at 8477 East Mud Lake Road, on the left. The trail begins at the parking lot. GPS: N43 10.809' / W76 24.137'

The Hike

One of the Syracuse area's most satisfying hiking experiences awaits you at Beaver Lake, where the nature center provides enough habitat diversity to attract more than 200 bird species, hundreds of plant species, and all of central New York's most common mammals.

A 200-acre lake forms the centerpiece of this natural space, while hardwood forest, open meadows, and a wetland bog surround the lake. The Lake Loop hike traverses all of these habitats, bringing you closer to songbirds and waterfowl, squirrels and chipmunks, and a landscape that changes with the seasons, offering you wide views in winter and early spring and protecting nesting species in spring and summer.

The carefully maintained trail leads to a lengthy boardwalk through the reeds and willows on the lake's north side, where you can explore the marshland without wading through mud and muck. Watch here for red-winged blackbirds that scold as they try to draw your attention away from the reedy areas—they almost certainly have nests nearby. A muskrat may swim past with only a nose above the water, and Canada geese arrive by the thousands in the fall to rest and feed before heading to warmer climates.

As you come into the home stretch on the Lake Loop Trail, a short connecting path leads to the Three Meadows Trail. You may wish to detour and enjoy this loop, which winds through wildflower-rich open land loaded with grassland birds like savannah and song sparrows, blackbirds, eastern meadowlarks, and occasional bobolinks. Watch for northern harriers swooping over the field as they pursue their supper, and for short-eared owls hunting at dusk in the winter months.

Beaver Lake Nature Center: Lake Loop Trail

0 Kilometer 0.3

0 Mile 0.3

N

East Mud Lake Road

Deep Woods Trail

Woodland Trail

West Mud Lake Road

Lean-To

Beaver Lake

Observation Platform

Three Meadows Loop Trail

Vann Road

Miles and Directions

0.0 Start by walking across the lot to the Lake Loop trailhead. If you are facing the visitor center, the well-marked trailhead is to your right.

0.2 An unmarked trail goes off to the left. Continue straight.

0.3 The Woodland Trail crosses here. Continue straight.

0.4 The Woodland Trail crosses the Lake Loop again. Keep going straight.

0.6 The Deep Woods Trail crosses the loop. Stay straight on the Lake Loop.

0.7 The boardwalk through the wetland begins.

0.8 This is a great spot for a wide view of Beaver Lake.

1.1 The boardwalk ends and the packed dirt trail resumes.

1.3 The trail to the right goes to a log hut—a lean-to used in nature center programs. Continue straight.

1.7 Reach another boardwalk, shorter than the first.

1.8 The boardwalk ends. Reach another short boardwalk in about 300 feet.

2.1 There's an observation platform to your right, at a level with Vann Road. You can see an unofficial but well-worn trail up to the platform. The expansive water view to your left is what you will see from the platform. About 300 feet ahead, the trail crosses a service road. Continue straight.

2.4 Reach the connecting trail to the Three Meadows Trail loop to your right. Continue straight.

2.9 You've nearly reached the parking area. Turn left; the Three Meadows trailhead is to your right. The parking lot is visible ahead and to the right. To the left is the visitor center, where the trail officially ends. Walk the last 500 feet to the visitor center (which has a great gift shop) to complete the loop.

3.0 Arrive at the visitor center.

2 Clark Reservation State Park

Choose an easy amble through a quiet wood or a more rugged hike along a limestone outcropping above a deep, glacially carved lake.

Distance: 2.2-mile loop
Approximate hiking time: 1.25 hours
Difficulty: More challenging
Trail surface: Packed dirt trail, limestone rock
Best season: Apr through Nov
Other trail users: None
Canine compatibility: A maximum of two leashed dogs per party is permitted. You may be asked for proof of rabies inoculation. Pets are not permitted in/on playgrounds, buildings, boardwalks, or guarded beaches.
Fees and permits: Entrance fee per vehicle on weekends and holidays from Memorial Day to Labor Day; annual pass available
Schedule: Open daily, sunrise to sunset

Maps: www.parks.ny.gov/documents/parks/ClarkReservationTrailMap.pdf
Water availability: Drinking fountain outside the nature center
Trail contact: Clark Reservation State Park, 6105 East Seneca Tpke., Jamesville 13078; (315) 492-1590; https://parks.ny.gov/parks/clarkreservation/details.aspx
Finding the trailhead: From Syracuse take I-481 South to the Jamesville exit (exit 2). Turn left and take Jamesville Road south 1.3 miles to NY 173. Turn right onto NY 173 and continue 1.25 miles to the park entrance. The trail begins at the nature center, just off the parking area. GPS: N42 59.700' / W76 05.652'

The Hike

Named a "reservation" because the government set the land aside for Revolutionary War veterans back in 1792, this dramatically beautiful state park never passed to the heroes of that time—none of them claimed their share—but it managed to escape lasting development before it became parkland in 1926. Today we can enjoy the extraordinary scene created by glaciers some 10,000 to 20,000 years ago, laced with hints of the shallow sea that covered most of the continent hundreds of millions of years earlier.

Glacier Lake, one of the park's most significant landmarks, is a glacial plunge pool—a deep bowl carved by torrents of meltwater as glaciers of the last ice age receded from this area. The lake is 62 feet deep, and its surface water does not mix with its bottom water, making this one of only a handful of meromictic lakes in the United States. The result is an astonishing clarity that allows visitors to see what lies below the surface in remarkable detail.

Your hike can be an easy walk along the Mildred Faust Trail or a more challenging trek along the Lake Trail to the Cliff Trail, with a 330-foot change in elevation in a brief 0.2-mile incline. The Faust Trail leads through woodland in which you may see any number of the 300 fern and flowering plant species documented here, as well as more than eighty tree and shrub varieties. Wildflowers abound here in spring and summer, and trees come into bloom in mid-May, filling the air with their fragrances.

The Lake Trail, a flat but rugged hike, follows the northern shore of Glacier Lake over rocks and fallen trees along a dirt path. The trail climbs quickly to the Cliff Trail, from which you can enjoy a spacious view of the thick forest across the water and the deeply turquoise lake below. You'll traverse a series of limestone slabs along the cliff's edge and climb several short stone stairways to reach the highest point on the trail (at about 740 feet). From here the trail becomes easy again as you follow the Faust Trail into the woods and back to the parking area.

Miles and Directions

0.0 Start at the nature center and take the stairs down to the Lake Trail (177 steps in all). At the bottom of the stairs, turn left onto the Lake Trail.

0.1 Follow the Lake Trail along Glacier Lake. The trail is rocky but fairly level and well blazed with green paint on the trees. The path provides terrific views of the lake—look at the edges, where you can see entire trees that have fallen into the water as the earth eroded under their roots.

0.7 Reach the top of the only major incline on this part of the trail. Continuing straight will take you to a power line right-of-way that stands at the edge of the park; if you've reached the power lines, you've gone too far. Turn around to your left and follow the Cliff Trail. In about 450 feet the Saddle Back Trail goes to your right. Continue straight.

0.9 Take the steps up to the limestone ledge. Look left for great views of the lake and the distant forest. The path is wide, but there's no railing here; take care as you walk.

1.0 The Long Trail goes off to the right. Continue straight.

1.2 Reach the last great overlook point before you leave the Cliff Trail. Take time to enjoy the view before turning right onto the Big Buck Trail.

1.4 The Big Buck Trail intersects the Dry Lake Trail. Continue straight.

1.5 Turn right onto the Mildred Faust Trail loop.

1.8 Turn right to begin the return route on the Faust Trail.

2.0 The trail turns sharply left, then right. Pass the Dry Lake Trail junction to your left and continue on the Table Rock Trail. In about 450 feet the Table Rock Trail goes left. Continue straight.

2.1 Cross a boardwalk.

2.2 Turn right and continue to the parking area, which you will reach in about 350 feet.

3 Pratt's Falls Park

A quick descent to a rushing cascade followed by an easy walk through a cool woods make this a great little hike for families with children.

Distance: 0.9-mile loop
Approximate hiking time: 30 minutes
Difficulty: Easy, with some stairs
Trail surface: Packed dirt trail, rock stairs
Best season: Apr and May, Sept and Oct
Other trail users: None
Canine compatibility: Leashed dogs permitted
Fees and permits: Admission per vehicle
Schedule: Apr through Aug, 7 a.m. to 8:30 p.m.; Sep and Oct, sunrise to sunset. Closed Nov through Mar.

Maps: www.onondagacounty parks.com/assets/Uploads /PrattsFallsMap2017.pdf
Water availability: Restrooms in parking area in season or at the park office
Trail contact: Pratt's Falls Park, 7671 Pratt's Falls Rd., Man- lius 13104; (315) 683-5550; https://onondagacountyparks .com/parks/pratts-falls-park
Finding the trailhead: From US 20 in Pompey, take Henneberry Road north 2 miles to CR 218 (Pratt's Falls Road). Turn right onto CR 218 and continue to the park entrance. The trail begins at the parking area. GPS: N42 55.899' / W75 59.589'

The Hike

If you're heading into the forested country south of Syracuse for a picnic or a grand day out, Pratt's Falls is a must-see stop: This park features a 137-foot ribbon cascade falls with a viewing platform that brings you close enough to feel the fresh-water spray when the waterfall is at its fullest in spring.

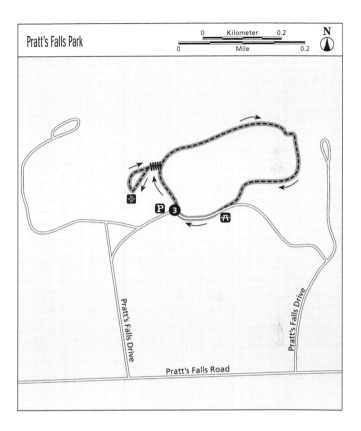

Pratt's Falls served area residents well in the days before European settlers' arrival, providing a plentiful water supply and fishing for the Seneca people who made their home in and around this park. Later the falls became the site of the first mill in Onondaga County, providing power for a sawmill as early as 1796, and later a gristmill as well.

The brief walk down the steps to the waterfall only whets visitors' appetites for more of the park, so consider this short hike once you've ascended the stairs, especially if you have children who will enjoy a little more time in the woods before or after your picnic.

The trail leads along the Limestone Creek gorge and through hardwood forest, then away from the creek as it arcs farther into the woods. In a few minutes the trail emerges at the edge of a picnic area, looping back along the edge of the woods to the parking area.

If you're looking for a longer hike, the North Rim trail is a 2.6-mile loop that explores a much larger section of the park. Find more about this route on the map at the link provided earlier in the hike details.

Miles and Directions

0.0 Start at the parking area and look for the gateway sign that says FALLS TRAIL. Pass under this sign to the stairs and descend to the first level. Turn left to proceed down the ramp to the stairs that lead to the falls (seventy-seven stairs in all).

0.2 At the bottom of the stairs, the Falls Overlook provides the best head-on view of Pratt's Falls. On sunny days, watch for rainbows in the spray above the cascading waters. Return up the stairs to the junction with the rest of the trail.

0.3 Go straight to continue the trail loop.

0.7 The trail follows a level path through the forest, emerging here at the edge of the picnic area. Turn left or right to continue along the woods' edge to your picnic table or to the parking area.

0.9 Complete the loop by returning to the parking lot and your vehicle.

4 Green Lakes State Park

Two deep, turquoise lakes, an old-growth forest, and a veritable festival of wildflowers and wildlife combine to make this one of the most popular easy hikes in the Syracuse area.

Distance: 3.1-mile loop
Approximate hiking time: 1.5 hours
Difficulty: Easy
Trail surface: Packed dirt trail, some paved sections
Best season: Apr through Nov
Other trail users: Joggers, cross-country skiers, cyclists
Canine compatibility: Up to two leashed dogs permitted per group. Pets are not permitted in playgrounds or buildings, or on boardwalks or beaches.
Fees and permits: Entry fee per vehicle
Schedule: Open daily, dawn to dusk

Maps: https://www.parks.ny.gov /documents/parks/GreenLakes TrailMap.pdf
Water availability: Restrooms in parking area or at clubhouse
Trail contact: Green Lakes State Park, 7900 Green Lakes Rd., Fayetteville 13066; (315) 637-6111; https://parks.ny.gov /parks/greenlakes/details.aspx
Finding the trailhead: From Syracuse take I-690 East 7 miles to NY 290 East. Continue on NY 290 for 10 miles to the park entrance at Green Lakes Road. After the ticket booth, park in the area near Green Lake Beach. GPS: N43 03.489' / W75 57.879'

The Hike

Few central New York hikes pack as much fascinating geology, beautiful scenery, and accessible wildlife watching into one walk as does Green Lakes State Park—so it's no wonder that this park attracts visitors from all over the area to circle its lakes on foot, on skis, or by bicycle. As lovely as it is geologically significant, Green Lakes offers an easy walk with enough length and variation to hold a hiker's interest over and over again.

The two lakes—sometimes a bright turquoise, sometimes emerald green—credit their vibrant color to a combination of factors. About 15,000 years ago, a massive waterfall created by glacial meltwater pounded this area, sculpting the deep lakes you see here and a handful of others, including Glacier Lake in Clark Reservation State Park. This forceful formation caused the lakes to become meromictic: While most lakes experience a turnover of their waters with the temperature changes of spring and fall, pulling silts from the lower waters up to the surface, Green and Round Lakes do not turn over. The result is the eerie clarity you see here— with objects well below the surface standing out in sharp relief—and the resulting light penetration produces the saturated shades of emerald and cyan.

This hike takes you around both lakes, crossing between them along a merry stream that connects their waters. As you leave Green Lake and begin your circuit of Round Lake, stop to admire Round Lake's color and its idyllic setting. In 1973 this 170-foot-deep lake was designated a National Natural Landmark by the National Park Service as one of only a few meromictic lakes of this depth in the United States. The adjacent one hundred acres of old-growth forest contain trees that are hundreds of years old. You can explore this area further on the Old Growth Trail, a loop that leads away from Round Lake from the lake's southwest side.

Such an exciting landscape naturally attracts all manner of wildlife, from the ubiquitous chipmunks to white-tailed deer, as well as migrating warblers, wood thrush, woodpeckers

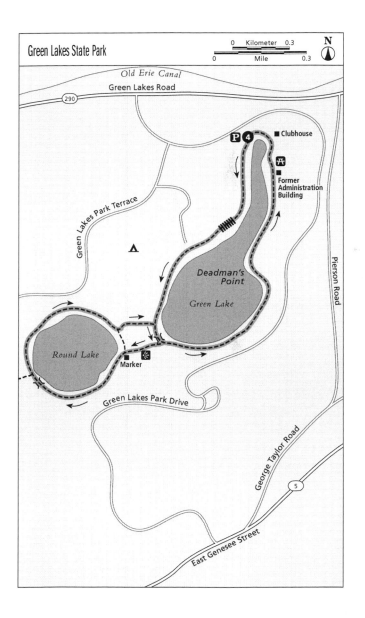

Green Lakes State Park

0   Kilometer   0.3

0   Mile   0.3

N

Old Erie Canal

Green Lakes Road

290

Green Lakes Park Terrace

Clubhouse

P 4

Former
Administration
Building

Deadman's
Point

Green Lake

Round Lake

Marker

Green Lakes Park Drive

Pierson Road

George Taylor Road

5

East Genesee Street

(including the magnificent pileated woodpecker), cedar wax-wing, and many others.

As you come into the last leg of this trail, don't miss Deadman's Point, an actual reef—like you'd find under the ocean—created by a buildup of a calcium carbonate substance called marl. Bacteria produce the marl on an ongoing basis, expanding the reef as it encrusts algae, mosses, and even fallen trees. This striking sight makes for a weirdly pretty underwater-scape on the edge of Green Lake.

Miles and Directions

0.0 Start at the Green Lake Beach parking area. The trail begins as a paved path.

0.2 The pavement ends and the trail surface becomes crushed stone and a groomed dirt path.

0.4 Pass a set of wooden stairs going up the hill to your right. Continue straight.

0.8 Take the cross trail to your left to continue to Round Lake. This little trail takes you past the stream that connects the two lakes.

0.9 Cross the bridge over the connecting stream and turn right.

1.0 The path to the right goes to a platform overlooking the stream. Stop here before continuing to Round Lake. You'll reach the lake in about 300 feet. A marker here explains Round Lake's National Natural Landmark status.

1.4 Reach a bridge over a low spot that affords a terrific view of the lake through the trees. You can see entire trees that have collapsed into the lake here. In a few feet you'll come to the junction with the Old Growth Trail. If you'd like to take this short loop trail, turn left. Otherwise continue on the Round Lake Trail. As you come around the western side of the lake, the park's high hills rise on your left. Watch the understory for ground-feeding thrushes and sparrows.

1.9 The trail goes straight and to the left. To complete the figure eight, turn left onto the connector trail.

2.0 Turn right to complete the loop around the east side of Green Lake. Continue straight on this trail around the lake.

2.5 You've reached Deadman's Point, which is easy to see at any time but is at its most vivid when lake levels are lower in summer and fall. When you're ready, continue on the trail around the lake.

2.7 A trail to the right leads to a picnic area. Continue straight. The large building ahead to the right is the former administration building, constructed in the 1930s by the Civilian Conservation Corps.

2.9 The trail reaches the paved pathway around the clubhouse and the beach. Continue on the paved path to the parking area.

3.1 Arrive back at the parking area.

5 Chittenango Falls State Park

Descend into a gorge for head-on views of a 167-foot water-fall, then meander through woods and meadows filled with fruit trees and flowering shrubs.

Distance: 2.2-mile loop
Approximate hiking time: 1.25 hours
Difficulty: Easy
Trail surface: Packed dirt trail, some paved sections, stone and wooden stairs
Best season: Apr through Nov
Other trail users: Cross-country skiers
Canine compatibility: Leashed dogs permitted
Fees and permits: Entrance fee in season
Schedule: The park is open daily from dawn to dusk, but the Gorge Trail is only open from late spring to late fall. Call the park to check on trail closures.
Maps: https://www.parks.ny.gov /documents/parks/Chittenango FallsTrailMap.pdf

Water availability: Restrooms in parking area
Trail contact: Chittenango Falls State Park, 2300 Rathbun Rd., Cazenovia 13035; (315) 492-1756; https://parks.ny.gov /parks/chittenangofalls/details .aspx
Finding the trailhead: From Syracuse take I-481 South to exit 3E toward Fayetteville. Turn right onto East Genesee Street/NY 5 and follow NY 5 east for 10.4 miles to Route 13 South. Turn right on NY 13 South and travel 6 miles to the park entrance, which will be on your right. The trail begins at the parking lot. GPS: N42 58.696' / W75 50.577'

The Hike

Begin at the top of one of central New York's hidden gems, where Chittenango Falls tumbles an impressive 167 feet over a series of ridges in the north-flowing Chittenango Creek. Whether it's a leisurely trickle in the heat of summer or a rushing torrent in early May, this waterfall reveals more than 400 million years of geologic history behind its descending waters.

Many eons ago, when a shallow sea covered the land that would become North America, limestone and dolomite rocks formed as silt, sand, and other sediments drifted with the water to the sea's floor. You can see the layers of these early rock formations in the stratified sedimentary wall behind the falls. Observant hikers may find fossils in the rocks along the creek and throughout the park, the remnants of aquatic creatures that made their home in that primordial sea.

In addition to all that remains from prehistoric times, Chittenango Falls State Park provides a breeding ground for contemporary animals and plants as well. The Chittenango ovate amber snail—a tiny critter less than an inch long that thrives on the slopes alongside the waterfall—lives only in this park and nowhere else in the world. Fewer than twenty-five of these snails existed as recently as 1990.

See if you can spot roseroot, an endangered flowering plant that lives here in the park and in only two other places in New York State. It clings to high, sheer ledges in the gorge near the falls along with Hart's-tongue fern, which loves rocky environments with consistent moisture. Bring binoculars to get a good look at both of these plants in spring and summer.

Your hike takes you down into the gorge for magnificent head-on views of the falls and the roiling creek at its base, so bring your camera: By the time you reach the bottom of the stone and wooden staircases that lead into the gorge, you'll stand on a pedestrian bridge that places the falls front and

Chittenango Falls State Park

CHITTENANGO FALLS STATE PARK

Rathbun Road

Chittenango Creek

ME

Gorge Road

CH

Pedestrian Bridge

Falls Overlook

5

Rathbun Road

Rathbun Road

0 — Kilometer — 0.2
0 — Mile — 0.2

N

center for your photographic enjoyment. Then it's back up the steps to explore a section of the park that receives less attention but provides a solid hike through forest, meadows, and hedgerows of wild flowering shrubs.

Miles and Directions

0.0 Start at the parking lot. Walk to the paved footpath and turn right to reach the overlook at the top of the falls. When you're ready to continue, you'll see the path to the lower overlook points on your right. Start down the stairs.

0.1 Reach the middle overlook, with your first head-on view of the falls. Continue down the stairs to the pedestrian bridge.

0.2 Walk out on the pedestrian bridge for the best view of the falls yet. If it is open, you can cross the bridge and return to the top of the gorge using the Gorge Trail. If it isn't, go back up the stairs the way you came.

0.4 You are back at the top of the stairs. Take the paved path and continue until you see the sign for the Chips Trail (the CH trail on the park's map) in about 250 feet. Turn right onto this trail, cross the bridge over the wash, and continue straight as you follow the yellow trail markers.

0.7 Turn right at this intersection. Continue to follow the yellow trail markers.

0.8 The trail goes two ways here: straight and up to the left. Go straight across the bridge over a stream. You'll cross another bridge shortly, and then the trail splits. Go straight up the hill.

0.9 Several trails meet here. You'll see green trail markers here for the park's Meadow Trail—the MD trail on the park map. Follow these to the left.

1.0 Take the trail to the right over the bridge. From here follow the bright-orange plastic trail markers you'll see on sticks, indicating the Meadow Trail Extension (ME) trail. In about

250 feet you'll cross another bridge, then emerge in a meadow that also serves as the electrical right-of-way for the local power company. A steady incline leads to the next intersection.

1.3 The trail turns left. Continue straight to the next intersection.

1.4 Turn left and cross the bridge and begin a steep incline to an open meadow. In the meadow, go straight through the next intersection.

1.5 Follow the green plastic markers for the Meadow Trail (the park's MD trail). The orange trail ends here. The green trail goes straight and left. Take the left.

1.6 Continue straight, up and around through the swamp grass, up over the knoll, and down into the wooded area.

1.7 Travel through the wooded area, carefully crossing the creek.

1.8 When the trail reaches a T, turn right and link back with the yellow trail.

2.1 At the intersection with the road, keep left. About 250 feet straight ahead, the trail leads to private property. Turn left to stay in the park, and cross the footbridge. In another 150 feet turn left to reach the restrooms, or turn right to continue to the parking lot. Cross the bridge over the wash into the developed area of the park.

2.2 Arrive back at the parking lot and the starting point of the trail.

6 Stone Quarry Hill Art Park

Art meets nature among the meadows, hedgerows, and woodlands of this quirky space, each made greater by sweeping views of the countryside.

Distance: 1.5-mile loop
Approximate hiking time: 45 minutes
Difficulty: Easy
Trail surface: Packed dirt, mowed grass, some crushed gravel
Best season: Apr through Nov
Other trail users: Cross-country skiers, snowshoers
Canine compatibility: Leashed dogs permitted
Fees and permits: Donation suggested
Schedule: Open daily, dawn to dusk
Maps: https://sqhap.org/visit
Water availability: No running water onsite. Composting toilets are available at the top of the hill Apr through Oct.

Trail contact: Stone Quarry Hill Art Park, 3883 Stone Quarry Rd., PO Box 251, Cazenovia 13035; (315) 655-3196; https://sqhap.org
Special considerations: Please do not climb on artworks.
Finding the trailhead: From Syracuse take I-690 East to I-481 South to exit 3E toward Fayetteville. Follow NY 92 for 12.7 miles to US 20. Turn left onto US 20 and follow it to Stone Quarry Road; turn right. Pass the buildings and park in the gravel lot at the top of the hill. Begin the hike at the Vista trailhead. GPS: N42 54.668' / W75 50.056'

The Hike

This quirky little 104-acre park hosts a variety of outdoor art, created and installed by emerging and established artists from all over the country. Exhibitions feature new works every year, many of which you will discover as you walk the easy, rolling trails. Come in the summer and view work in any number of media, from recycled materials to cast concrete, each appearing in the woods or on the hilltop. Even the trees and shrubs become part of the art using intriguing labels, a particularly appropriate cluster of trunks, or an appealing setting to turn the natural into the intentional.

The hike travels through alternating meadows, tight woodlands, and formerly tilled fields, establishing a patchwork of outdoor spaces in regular sequence. Begin on the Vista Trail with the panoramic view that gives the trail its name—a vast green and gold countryside in New York's Finger Lakes region.

Your hike follows the Woodland Trail, the Secret Garden Trail (which oddly does not actually feature a garden), and the Hawthorn and Old Quarry Trails, climaxing in an equally compelling viewpoint to the north. The final leg swings up between the meadow's edge and the hedgerow, finally rejoining the Secret Garden Trail and ending at the Vista once again.

To extend your park experience, pick up a nature brochure at the hilltop kiosk or, on weekends, in the Studio Gift Shop (open Friday through Sunday, noon to 5 p.m. during the exhibition season), and explore the other 3 miles of trails.

As in many other small parks, trails crisscross one another and beg to lead you astray at nearly every intersection. If you keep the hilltop as your North Star, you will find your way back even if you wander onto one of the outer trails (Watershed or Meadow View).

Most important, be sure to make the turn off the Link Trail (blue markers)—part of the venerable Finger Lakes Trail and a connecting path for the North Country National Scenic Trail. The North Country Trail begins in eastern upstate

New York and continues all the way to North Dakota, covering 625 miles in New York State alone and more than 2,000 miles along its full length. While you may yearn to tackle a long-distance trail, that's probably not why you've come to Stone Quarry Hill—so be sure to make the turn onto the Secret Garden Trail at the 0.3-mile point.

Miles and Directions

0.0 Start on the gravel path that begins at the southern end of the parking lot. You'll see a sign for the Vista Trail. As you walk from here, the wide-angle view of New York's southern tier comes into view.

0.1 Enter the woods. Note the double blue markers on a tree at the edge of the woods. The Link Trail is the blue trail; follow this for now. In about 250 feet a trail goes off to the left. Continue straight.

0.2 Follow the orange marker for the Woodland Trail to the left. Soon you will see a blue marker for the Link Trail, going to the right. Turn right. (The Woodland Trail continues straight.)

0.3 Turn left at the meadow. In about 250 feet enter the woods and begin the Secret Garden Trail. Follow the blue marker to the left at the next intersection, then go straight and follow the Secret Garden loop. In a few steps, a narrow wooden plank system covers a wet spot. Continue straight.

0.4 At the pavilion in the clearing, turn left and pick up the path at the woods. You'll pass a pond on the way. The next intersection comes up quickly; turn left at the Old Quarry Trail sign and follow the white markers. Soon you'll emerge in a meadow—continue straight and reenter the woods. Then turn right onto the Hawthorn Trail.

0.7 At the intersection with the Watershed Trail, turn right and return to the meadow. Turn left onto the meadow edge and follow the mowed path. From here the trail begins a series of steady but gradual inclines, rising to a great view of

Cazenovia Lake to the southwest and the hilly terrain to the south.

1.0 The Old Quarry Trail goes right; continue straight through the hedgerow and along another meadow. Turn right at the woods and continue along the hedgerow.

1.2 Reach a parking lot and gravel path to the road on your left. (Option: For a shortcut back to your car, turn left and walk along the road.) Continue straight to pick up the Secret

Garden Trail again. In about 450 feet you'll reenter the woods on the Secret Garden Trail.

1.3 Turn left and walk straight across the meadow on the mowed path, up the last incline before the parking lot.

1.4 Turn left at the gravel path and walk around the rest of the Vista Trail for some northern views before returning to your vehicle.

1.5 Arrive back at the parking lot.

7 Montezuma National Wildlife Refuge: South Spring Pool and Esker Brook Trails

This quiet ramble follows a glacially created ridge through a hardwood forest that echoes with birdsong, ending at a tranquil wetland pond.

Distance: Three trails provide options for a 3-mile hike and/or several shorter routes

Approximate hiking time: 1.5 hours

Difficulty: Easy

Trail surface: Dirt path, mowed grass in one long section

Best season: Apr through June, Sept through Nov

Other trail users: Birders

Canine compatibility: Leashed dogs permitted

Fees and permits: No fees or permits required

Schedule: Open daily, dawn to dusk. All Esker Brook Trails and South Spring Pool Trail close during white-tailed deer hunting season (Nov 1–mid-Dec)

Maps: www.fws.gov/sites /default/files/documents/ montezuma-public-use-map -2021.pdf

Water availability: At the visitor center; open Apr 1 through Oct 31, 10 a.m. to 3 p.m. weekdays, until 4 p.m. weekends; weekends only in Nov; closed Dec through Mar

Trail contact: Montezuma National Wildlife Refuge, 3395 US 20 East, Seneca Falls 13148; (315) 568-5987; www.fws.gov /r5mnwr

Special considerations: Insect repellent a must from May through mid-Sept

Finding the trailhead: From Syracuse, take the New York Thruway (I-90) West to exit 40 (Weedsport). Turn right at NY 34 and right again at NY 31. Continue 10.6 miles and turn left onto NY 89 (Armitage Road). Drive about

1.5 miles and turn left onto Wiley Road (continue to follow NY 89). Pass the Tschache Pool parking area, cross over the Thruway, and turn right onto East Tyre Road. Continue to the Esker Brook Trails parking area and trailhead. GPS: N42 58.452' / W76 47.030'

The Hike

Three trails follow this edge of Montezuma National Wildlife Refuge, a protected wetland since 1938 and one of the most popular landing grounds in upstate New York for tens of thousands of Canada and snow geese, ducks, gulls, and terns every spring and fall. Esker Brook Trails skirt the western edge of the refuge, which offers shelter and plentiful feeding to migrating songbirds throughout the months of April, May, September, and October.

Your walk begins on the Ridge Trail, leading into a forest of leafy hardwoods with a dense understory of berry-bearing shrubs, which produce their brilliant fruit in late summer and fall. Ferns, broadleaf groundcover, and wildflowers effectively obscure the forest floor from late April until the leaves fall in early November. Soon you make a right turn onto the South Spring Pool Trail, one of the most productive routes in the refuge for birding during spring and fall migration. The South Spring route provides a flat, easy out-and-back trail where you can scout for warblers, vireos, waxwings, and other passerines with predictable success.

When you return to the Ridge Trail, you may find yourself eye to eye with a thrilling variety of warblers in spring—black-and-white, Blackburnian, black-throated blue and green, Nashville, chestnut-sided, bay-breasted, magnolia, Canada, Wilson's, Tennessee, and even occasional Connecticut warblers light here on their way to parts north in May or south in September. Vireos, thrushes, and sparrows can be thick in these woods during the migration and mating seasons, and you are certain to encounter tight flocks of ruby-crowned kinglets in early May, probably fraternizing with black-capped chickadees and tufted titmice.

The Ridge Trail then reveals the neighboring countryside, crossing the edge of an open field filled with wildflowers in spring and summer and alive with bird activity. The trail terminates as it reaches two ponds, favorite places for swimming muskrats as well as belted kingfishers, green and great blue herons, and wood ducks. As you circle the ponds in the third segment of your walk, watch along the edges of the reeds for common moorhens and elusive Virginia rails. Spring peepers will fill the air with their song on warm days in April, and hawks—including the ospreys and bald eagles that nest in the refuge—may pass overhead.

When you've returned almost to your starting point after your pond loop, take the Orchard or Brook Trail back through the woods. You'll be closer to the forest floor on either trail, following the brook at the bottom of the esker. Here you have a better view of the wildflowers and other plant life that form the area's ample understory, making this the best place to watch for ground-feeding birds like thrushes and white-crowned and white-throated sparrows, as well as eastern cottontails, chipmunks, gray squirrels, and raccoons at dawn and dusk.

Miles and Directions

0.0 Start at the trailhead in the parking lot. Enter the woods at the Ridge Trail trailhead, at the west end of the lot. Cross a bridge over Esker Brook. As you enter the woods, the trail will take you to the left through the forest. The trail gives you an opportunity to look down into the forest to your right, a great

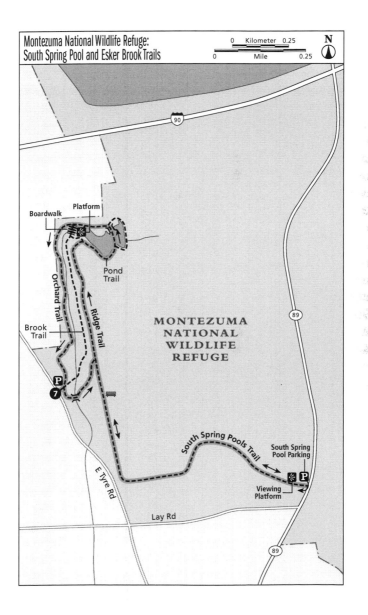

Montezuma National Wildlife Refuge:
South Spring Pool and Esker Brook Trails

0   Kilometer   0.25

0   Mile   0.25

N

Boardwalk

Platform

Pond Trail

Orchard Trail

Ridge Trail

Brook Trail

MONTEZUMA
NATIONAL
WILDLIFE
REFUGE

P
7

90

89

South Spring Pools Trail

South Spring Pool Parking

Viewing Platform

P

E Tyre Rd

Lay Rd

89

way to look for treetop-dwelling warblers, vireos, woodpeckers, jays, and other migrants.

0.1 The South Spring Pools Trail goes right here, leading through a wetland and out to NY 89. If you like, turn right onto the South Spring Pools Trail, and walk the mowed grass path with an open field full of red osier dogwood to your left. Pass a bench on your left.

0.4 The trail goes straight (out to NY 414) or to the left and down a small incline. Turn left to visit South Spring and its pools. From here, the grass path takes in the edges of the Montezuma wetland, with views of waterfowl and long-legged waders in spring and fall, and breeding ducks in summer.

1.0 Here is an observation platform with a bench, and the widest view of South Spring Pool. When you're done here, return up the mowed grass path to the Ridge Trail.

1.9 Enjoy the wide view of the countryside as you continue straight on the Ridge Trail.

2.3 The Pond Trail goes right; the Brook Trail goes left. Turn right. This part of the path is mowed grass and can be very wet in spring or after heavy rain. Watch for belted kingfishers, marsh wrens, and swamp sparrows as you circle the pond.

2.4 An indistinct trail to the right through the shrubs offers an opportunity to circle the second pond. The easier route crosses the dike straight ahead, with excellent viewing of both ponds. Continue straight. Look for great blue herons—a Montezuma staple—as well as elusive rails or bitterns in the tall grasses.

2.5 Reach a bridge over a brook—actually a connecting stream between the two ponds. After the bridge, trails go right (around the second pond) and left (return trails). Turn left onto the Orchard Trail. In about 300 feet a set of steps leads down to a pond-viewing platform.

2.6 The Brook and Orchard Trails split here. Each leads directly back to the parking area at different levels in the woods.

Take the Orchard Trail and watch for ground-feeding birds, chipmunks, squirrels, and frogs hopping across the path.

3.0 Turn right at the intersection and proceed straight ahead to the parking area. Before you leave the refuge, drive around the 3-mile Wildlife Drive loop, especially in May or October. Concentrations of ducks, grebes, geese, and gulls here reach National Geographic–style proportions during the spring and fall migration. When a peregrine falcon drifts over the flocks and they all take wing at once, it's a sight not to be missed.

8 Montezuma National Wildlife Refuge: Seneca Trail

Slow down your exploration of this magnificent wildlife refuge as you search on foot for shorebirds, warblers, and more.

Distance: 1-mile loop
Approximate hiking time: 40 minutes
Difficulty: Easy
Trail surface: Crushed stone path, some pavement
Best season: Apr through June, Sept through Nov
Other trail users: Birders
Canine compatibility: Leashed dogs permitted
Fees and permits: No fees or permits required
Schedule: Open daily, dawn to dusk
Maps: www.fws.gov/sites /default/files/documents /montezuma-public-use -map-2021.pdf
Water availability: At the visitor center; open Apr 1 through Oct 31, 10 a.m. to 3 p.m. weekdays, until 4 p.m. weekends; weekends only in Nov; closed Dec through Mar

Trail contact: Montezuma National Wildlife Refuge, 3395 US 20 East, Seneca Falls 13148; (315) 568-5987; www.fws.gov /r5mnwr
Special considerations: Insect repellent a must from May through mid-Sept
Finding the trailhead: From Syracuse, take the New York Thruway (I-90) west to exit 40 (Weedsport). Turn right at NY 34 and right again at NY 31. In about 8.5 miles, turn left onto NY 90 South. In 4.4 miles, turn right onto US 20 West. Turn right at the entrance to Montezuma National Wildlife Refuge. Drive up the entrance road to the Visitor Center, and park in the lot there. The Seneca Trailhead is at the north end of the parking area. GPS: N42 58.051' / W76 44.388'

The Hike

Most visitors to Montezuma National Wildlife Refuge come for the spectacular numbers of waterfowl and shorebirds that arrive every spring and fall as they migrate to and from their breeding grounds in northern Canada, but Montezuma also serves as a stopover for dozens of species of passerines—birds that perch in trees and shrubs. Warblers, vireos, thrushes, flycatchers, towhees, sparrows, grosbeaks, and many other birds find their way to Montezuma's wooded areas, stands of hardwoods wedged between the refuge's wetlands and the Cayuga-Seneca Canal.

The relatively new Seneca Trail provides access to one of these woods, where pileated woodpeckers excavate holes for nests in spring and a wide variety of passerines pause to rest and feed before heading farther north. The trail's 1-mile length is deceptive, as you will want to spend more time here than the half hour it takes to walk this flat, easy loop. A spring visit may yield 30 or more bird species, while a fall walk can reveal solitary sandpipers, greater and lesser yellowlegs, and dunlin on the exposed mudflat in the creek bed as you cross the Wildlife Drive.

From spring through fall, take advantage of the observation tower and the viewing platform at the beginning of the trail, as they both provide wide views of the Main Pool and the surrounding wetlands. From here you are very likely to spot bald eagles and other raptors hunting for prey, as well as a fascinating variety of ducks, swans, geese, and grebes. Keep an eye out for black terns, a bird that has returned to the refuge after a long absence, now that the refuge's wildlife biologists have restored the native aquatic plant life that sustains

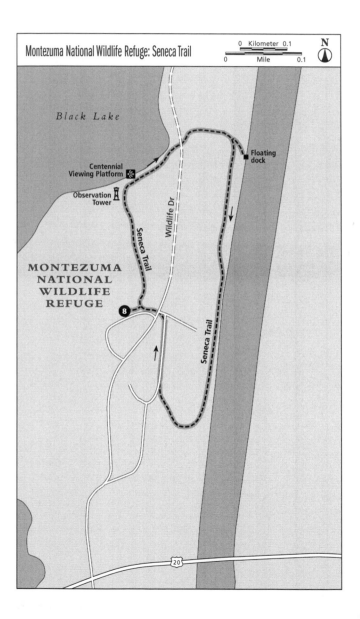

0   Kilometer   0.1

0   Mile   0.1

N

Black Lake

Centennial
Viewing Platform

Floating
dock

Observation
Tower

Wildlife Dr

Seneca Trail

MONTEZUMA
NATIONAL
WILDLIFE
REFUGE

8

Seneca Trail

20

these birds and so many others throughout the migration and breeding seasons.

Miles and Directions

0.0 Start at the trailhead at the northern end of the parking lot at the visitor center. Go straight, past the restrooms on your left.

0.1 The observation tower is here on the edge of the Main Pool.

0.2 Here is the viewing platform.

0.4 After you cross Wildlife Drive, proceed along the creek to the Cayuga-Seneca Canal. Stop at the floating dock if you'd like to enjoy the canal before continuing. From here, follow the canal on your left and the woods on your right.

0.6 The refuge's maintenance garage is on your right.

0.8 As the path curves right and away from the canal, an active osprey nest is at the top of the utility pole to the south.

0.9 The refuge office building is on your left. At the gravel path, turn right. Cross the Wildlife Drive.

1.0 Arrive back at the parking area.

9 Northern Montezuma WMA: Howland Island

With its wide trails, alternating meadows and shady woodlands, and a network of ponds that attracts thousands of migrating waterfowl, Howland Island is a wilderness paradise.

Distance: 5.7-mile lollipop
Approximate hiking time: 2.5 hours
Difficulty: Moderate due to length
Trail surface: Dirt and gravel roads
Best season: Apr through Nov
Other trail users: Cross-country skiers, cyclists, horseback riders
Canine compatibility: Leashed dogs permitted
Fees and permits: No fees or permits required
Schedule: Open daily, dawn to dusk
Maps: www.dec.ny.gov/docs /wildlife_pdf/nmontezuma4map .pdf
Water availability: None
Trail contact: DEC Region 8, 6274 E. Avon-Lima Rd., Avon,

NY 14414; (585) 226-5380; region8@dec.ny.gov
Special considerations: In summer wear a hat, sunscreen, and insect repellent.
Finding the trailhead: From Syracuse take the New York Thruway (I-90) west to exit 40. Follow NY 31 West and turn right onto NY 89. Continue on NY 89 to Savannah-Spring Lake Road and turn right. Follow Savannah-Spring Lake Road to Carncross Road. Turn left onto Carncross and continue until the road dead-ends at Howland Island. Park here and cross the bridge into the wildlife management area. GPS: N43 04.700' / W76 42.242'

The Hike

The Seneca River and the Erie Canal surround this 3,500-acre island, sequestering this patch of leafy woodlands, managed ponds, and open meadows and contributing to its preservation. Under the watchful management of the New York State Department of Environmental Conservation and a host of dedicated volunteers, this jewel in central New York's tiara provides one of the most appealing hiking experiences in the area—for those who are willing to take on some distance to reach its most compelling sections.

You'll walk a mile just to reach the first major intersection in the maintenance road network, but from here the marshes spread before you with their wealth of plant and animal life and their abundant bird populations. In late spring and throughout the summer, waterfowl can be hard to find. But in the fall, when leaves turn amber and cinnamon, the skies fill with V formations of Canada and snow geese, and migrating ducks arrive with the first gusts of north wind. By mid-September migrating warblers and vireos descend on the island in fallouts by the hundred, while thrushes flit through by night, their chip notes the only evidence of their stealthy passage.

Beyond its status as a birders' paradise, Howland Island serves up a colorful helping of spring and summer wildflowers and fall berries. Dame's rocket lines the roads with its nodding clusters of petals, while daylilies spring from gatherings of slender, dark green leaves on the roadside. Daisy fleabane, trillium, chicory, and Shasta daisy are just a few of the blooming varieties found here.

The second-growth forests provide long stretches of delightful shade, alternating with the meadows and cultivated fields, and edging the open ponds. Managed to provide habitat for migrating waterfowl and rare marsh birds, these ponds also furnish a breeding ground for turtles, many frog species, and those banes of every hiker's existence: mosquitoes and deer flies—and don't get me started on the deer ticks. Be sure to apply plenty of insect repellent before venturing into Howland Island, especially in the heat of summer. You may want to choose a cooler spring or fall day for this hike, as the bugs can be fierce when the air is humid.

Miles and Directions

0.0 Start from the parking area and walk past the yellow gate to the long, straight trail ahead. The trail is a dirt road through grassland dotted with small, excavated vernal ponds, alternating with stands of deciduous trees. An agricultural field opens out past the woods.

0.7 A dirt road goes right, into the field. This access road heads south to Hickory Hill. Continue straight.

1.0 A dirt road crosses here to the right and left. There's a storage building on the hill to your left. Continue straight; you'll come out on this road later, on the return route.

1.2 A road goes left here. You can see a marshy pond (Brooder Pond) ahead to the left. Continue straight down the dike past Brooder Pond.

1.6 The road forks to the left and right just past Brooder Pond. Take the road to the left. You'll have a nice view of CCC Pond just around the corner.

1.9 The path crosses a dike with Breeder Pond on the left. After the dike, Arum Pond appears on your right as you climb the hill to a meadow of tall grasses.

2.3 After a wooded section, Black Duck Pond appears on the left. You can still see Arum Pond on the right. Another access road goes right here; stay on the main trail and continue to your left around Black Duck Pond.

2.6 Turn left. Cook Pond is ahead on your right.

2.8 At Cook Pond the path goes straight and to the left. Continue straight.

3.5 A faint path goes right. Turn left. You are now on the road you crossed earlier, back at the 1.0-mile point.

4.7 Turn right at the intersection to head back to the parking area.

5.7 Arrive back at the entrance and parking area.

10 Seneca Meadows Wetland Preserve

There's no better place in central New York to look for American and least bittern on their breeding grounds—or to see acres of carefully maintained meadows filled with native wildflowers.

Distance: 3 miles

Approximate hiking time: 1.5 hours

Difficulty: Moderate for length

Trail surface: Crushed gravel

Best season: Apr through Nov

Other trail users: Bicyclists, cross-country skiers, snowshoers

Canine compatibility: Dogs permitted on leash

Fees and permits: No fees or permits required

Schedule: Open daily, dawn to dusk

Maps: www.senecameadows.com//wp-content/uploads/2020/03/Recreational_Trail-Map_15July2010.pdf

Water availability: Restrooms are available at the Seneca Meadows Environmental Education Center on NY 414 during open hours.

Trail contact: Seneca Meadows Landfill, 1786 Salcman Rd., Waterloo NY 13165; (315) 539-5624; https://senecameadows.com/wetlands-preserve

Special considerations: This trail is very exposed to the elements, with only a couple covered benches and a small path of woods to shield you from the sun. Wear a hat, bring plenty of water, and be sure to use sunscreen and bug repellent, especially during tick season.

Finding the trailhead: The preserve's street address is 1712 Black Brook Rd., Seneca Falls, NY 13148. From Syracuse, take I-90 (New York Thruway) to exit 41 for Waterloo. Turn right at the end of the ramp, and take NY 414 South 0.25 mile to NY 318. Turn left and continue on NY 318 for 1 mile. Turn right on Black Brook Road. Drive 1 mile to the preserve entrance on the right. GPS: N42 56.491' / W76 49.079'

The Hike

Good things can come out of waste mitigation projects, as Seneca Meadows Inc. demonstrates with this meticulously managed 576-acre wetland and forest project. Here the waste management and recycling company exceeded the requirement to preserve three times the acreage taken for industrial use, instead protecting eight times as much land as the company used for its Seneca Falls landfill. The result is the protection of 157 acres of existing wooded wetland and the creation of 419 acres of new wetland—a monumental task that resulted in a diverse series of ecosystems, from tall grass to wet prairie.

Here you can enjoy expansive areas filled with tall native plants, from black-eyed Susans to butterfly milkweed, as well as many species that have been crowded out of other open spaces by invasive plants. Abundant native flowers attract butterflies and native bees galore, and grassland birds, such as field, savannah, and song sparrows; swamp sparrow; marsh wren; and bobolink, frequent these areas in season. Ducks, including common merganser, American black duck, wood duck, and blue-winged teal, make the ponds here their summer breeding ground, and short-eared owls and rough-legged hawks can be seen hunting here in winter.

A walk around the 2.4-mile main loop trail provides good views of all of the preserve's ponds while surrounding foliage remains below eye level throughout the winter and in early spring. You can still get good looks at what's on the ponds in summer, though you may need to dodge some tall plant life to do so—and meanwhile, summer brings the

Seneca Meadows Wetland Preserve

0   Kilometer   0.25
0   Mile   0.25

N

Shed with bench ■   Main Trail

King Rd

P
10

ADA
Trail

Northern
Overlook ◄

White
Tail
Run

Oak Tree Pass Trail

Shed with bench/
Oak Tree Pass ■
Trailhead

Main Trail

Prairie
Overlook ◄

SENECA
MEADOWS
WETLAND
PRESERVE

Black Brook Rd

West Wood
Trail

Main Trail

Woods

Blue Heron Loop

butterflies, dragonflies, and fledgling birds learning to find their own food. Winter provides easier views of what's going on in the wooded areas, where woodpeckers and other hardy birds search for food under tree bark, and cedar waxwings and other fruit-eating birds feed on fermented berries.

Miles and Directions

0.0 From the parking area, take the ADA Trail. Come to the junction with White Tail Run, and continue right on the ADA Trail. In about 10 steps, go left on White Tail Run and continue to the Main Trail.

0.3 Turn right onto the Main Trail.

0.4 The Northern Overlook platform is to your left. Stop here for a nice view of the meadows.

0.5 Here is another junction with the ADA Trail. Continue straight on the Main Trail.

0.6 Here's a shed with a bench. There's no other shade on this trail, so it's a welcome respite.

1.2 Another shed with a bench marks the trailhead for Oak Tree Pass Trail. If you like, you can cut your hike in half here by taking Oak Tree Pass Trail across the preserve. Otherwise, continue on the Main Trail.

1.4 The West Wood Trail goes off to your right here. Continue straight.

1.6 A small area of trees provides the only other shade you will encounter on this trail.

1.7 The Blue Heron Loop trail begins here. If you want to walk around the large pond to your right, it adds about a mile to your hike.

2.0 Here's where the Blue Heron Loop comes out on the Main Trail.

2.5 A trail to the left leads to the Prairie Overlook.

2.7 The Oak Tree Pass Trail rejoins the Main Trail here. Continue straight.

2.8 You've completed the loop and returned to White Tail Run. Turn right. Bear right at the first intersection with the ADA Trail, and left at the second one.

3.0 You've reached the parking area and your vehicle.

11 Baltimore Woods Nature Center: Boundary Trail

Circle this charming woodland on a trail through open meadows filled with wildflowers and a cool forest alive with birds and chipmunks.

Distance: 2.7-mile loop

Approximate hiking time: 1.25 hours

Difficulty: Moderate

Trail surface: Dirt path

Best season: Apr through Nov

Other trail users: None

Canine compatibility: No dogs permitted

Fees and permits: No fees or permits required; donations encouraged

Schedule: Open daily, dawn to dusk

Maps: www.baltimorewoods.org/wp-content/uploads/2022/10/Baltimore-Woods-Nature-Center-Trails-2022_compressed.pdf

Water availability: At visitor center Mon through Fri, 9 a.m. to 4 p.m.; Sat 10 a.m. to 4 p.m.

Trail contact: Baltimore Woods Nature Center, 4007 Bishop Hill Rd., Marcellus, NY 13108; (315) 673-1350; www.baltimorewoods.org.

Finding the trailhead: From Syracuse take I-81 South to I-481 North and continue to exit 1 (Rock Cut Road/Brighton Avenue). At the light turn left onto NY 173 (West Seneca Turnpike). Continue 2.6 miles to NY 175 West. Pass through the town of Marcellus, and turn left onto South Street. At the Y in the road, bear right onto Bishop Hill Road (NY 211). Park in the lower parking area for Baltimore Woods. GPS: N42 57.943' / W76 20.633'

The Hike

This natural restoration of a former working farmland spans more than 180 acres with woods that feature hemlock as well as central New York's more typical maple, oak, tulip tree, beech, and northern white cedar. The center is not named for its previous owner, however: The story goes that the farmer decided to break with the local tradition of marketing his cattle in New York City, choosing to farm in this location because of its proximity to the railroad line to Baltimore. So well-known was he for this departure that people referred to his land as "Baltimore" . . . and the name stuck.

The loop trail around this mature hardwood forest introduces you to Baltimore Woods with a sampling of the nature center's scope, passing through forest and open field, down into the valley and across a creek, and out to the farmers' fields that flank the center's borders.

Spring and summer are excellent times to walk these woods, when red-eyed vireo and eastern wood-peewee call in alternating shifts and downy, hairy, and pileated woodpeckers rattle the trees with their drumming. Chipmunks dig their burrows right into the trail, popping their heads out and diving back in as your footsteps warn them of your arrival. Red and gray squirrels are a certain sighting, and there's a distinct possibility of spotting raccoon, fox, or deer, especially toward sunset.

Wildflowers fill the open fields with blue phlox, dame's rocket, Queen Anne's lace, and daisies, while mayapple blooms in the woods' understory and trillium pokes out from the leaf cover. Watch for wild strawberry in the grassy areas, and see if you can beat the birds and small animals to the berries in June.

Baltimore Woods Nature Center: Boundary Trail

Sand Pit Overlook

Sitting Area

New Seneca Turnpike

41

Boundary Trail

Field and Forest Trail

Valley Trail

Valley Trail

Mildred Faust Wildflower Garden

11

211

Bishop Hill

Miles and Directions

0.0 Start from the parking area and take the Valley Trail (yellow plastic markers on the trees) to the Boundary Trail. Walk in at the trailhead to the first post, and continue straight ahead onto the Valley Trail.

0.1 Reach the Mildred Faust Wildflower Garden, a cultivated garden that can help you identify flowers that are in bloom. Continue straight.

0.3 Turn right at the trail junction.

0.4 Cross the bridge over the creek. In a moment you'll reach the intersection with the Boundary Trail. Turn left, following the pink markers.

0.5 The Overlook Trail goes right here. Continue straight, following the Boundary Trail, and cross the creek again.

0.6 Reach another creek crossing. From here the trail gradually inclines as you come out of the woods into a more open area. Plenty of wildflowers find footing here. You'll reenter the woods in a bit.

0.9 The nature center's boundary is to the left; a farmer's plowed field reaches beyond. Continue straight on the path and enter a field of tall grasses. As the trail bends right, you'll enter a former orchard.

1.1 Ascend to the Sand Pit Overlook. The sand pit can be seen to your right—it's more of a ridge than a pit, from which sand erodes with wind and weather. Proceed through an open field along the park boundary and back into the woods. You'll walk along a ridge, with the brook babbling below you to the left.

1.4 As you descend from the ridge toward the forest floor, there's a sitting area with two benches overlooking the brook. You may want to stop here before you begin the next ascent from the valley.

1.9 Reach an intersection with the Field and Forest Trail. Continue straight on the Boundary Trail.

2.2 Come to a tricky intersection, just before you reach the center's other parking lot (not the one where you parked). Turn right and follow the Field and Forest Trail (green markers).

2.3 At the next intersection continue straight and follow the gray arrows to the visitor center.

2.4 Turn left at this intersection with the Valley Trail. You're now following a section of the Valley Trail that you did not hike earlier. Remember to follow the yellow markers now.

2.6 Cross a bridge over the brook and begin your final ascent out of the valley to the parking lot. Turn left at the power line right-of-way and continue to the parking area.

2.7 Arrive back at the visitor center and your vehicle.

12 Huckleberry Swamp

Lose yourself in the sounds and sights of nature in this 79-acre wetland preserve.

Distance: 0.7 mile loop
Approximate hiking time: 45 minutes
Difficulty: Easy
Trail surface: Mostly boardwalk with some woodland path
Best season: Apr through Nov
Other trail users: Birders
Canine compatibility: Leashed dogs permitted
Fees and permits: No fees or permits required
Schedule: Open daily from mid-April through mid-November, Tue through Sun, 7 a.m. to 7 p.m. Trail closes from end of November to mid-April.
Maps: https://www.waynecounty tourism.com/documents/Huckl Swamp.pdf
Water availability: None
Trail contact: Olga Fleisher Ornithological Foundation, PO Box 17718, Rochester, NY 14617; (585) 229-1050; www.ofofinc.org.
Special considerations: Huckleberry Swamp worked in conjunction with Forever Wild for

Everyone to design a trail here that is completely accessible to people with disabilities. This trail closes for the winter when the boardwalk gets slippery. It reopens in April when water levels do not cover the trail. Check the foundation's website or Facebook page to be sure the trail is open.

Finding the trailhead: The park's street address is 9190 Catchpole Rd., North Rose, NY. From Syracuse, take I-690 West to NY 690 North. In 5.7 miles, take the NY 31 East/NY 370 exit toward Baldwinsville. Merge onto NY 31 West/NY 370 West toward Meridian. Follow NY 370 West for 21 miles, and continue as it turns left and becomes Ridge Road. In 2.2 miles, turn left onto NY 104 West. Stay on 104 for 8.7 miles, and turn left onto Brick Schoolhouse Road. In 2.2 miles, turn right onto Catchpole Road. The preserve is on the left in about 0.5 mile. GPS: N43 10.285' / W76 56.772'

Huckleberry Swamp

Catchpole Rd

Boardwalk

12 P

Huckleberry Swamp Trail

Huckleberry Swamp Trail

Viewing platform with benches

Boardwalk

N

0   Kilometer   0.1
0   Mile   0.1

The Hike

Of the many kinds of wetlands preserved throughout New York State, this one is an actual swamp: a wet-bottomed forest of northern tree species, including elm, ash, and maple. This combination of fresh water and trees makes a visit to Huckleberry Swamp particularly appealing, with a sturdy, accessible boardwalk lifting you over the inundated areas and leading you through the forest.

The Olga Fleisher Ornithological Foundation maintains this preserve for birds and wildlife, so come with binoculars and be prepared to enjoy a wide variety of birds, especially in spring. Canada goose, wood duck, and mallards are ever-present residents; keep an eye out for great blue and green herons posing in the water as well. Trees here play host to all five local woodpeckers: red-bellied, downy, hairy, pileated, and northern flicker. Expect to hear—and maybe see—an Acadian flycatcher, as well as the more common willow, least, and great crested flycatcher; vireos abound here as well, so look for yellow-throated, warbling, red-eyed, and possible blue-headed vireos high in the trees. The flutelike song of the wood thrush and the veery's spiral harmonics pierce the evenings here, while common yellowthroat, American redstart, northern waterthrush, and yellow warbler all breed in the preserve. Watch for the red flash of a scarlet tanager or the bright magenta throat of the red-breasted grosbeak throughout the summer months.

Miles and Directions

0.0 There's only one trailhead at the parking area. Start down the dirt path.

0.1 The first stretch of boardwalk begins.

0.2 The first boardwalk ends. Continue on the path.

0.3 The second boardwalk starts here.

0.4 A viewing platform here provides a wide view of the swamp, as well as places to sit down.

0.6 The second boardwalk ends. The dirt path continues.

0.7 Arrive back at the parking area.

13 Chimney Bluffs State Park

Hike through an evergreen forest and along a high bluff to see the effects of wind, storm, and winter on this Great Lake ridgeline.

Distance: 2.2-mile loop
Approximate hiking time: 1 hour
Difficulty: Moderate
Trail surface: Dirt path
Best season: June through Sept
Other trail users: None
Canine compatibility: Leashed dogs permitted
Fees and permits: Entry fee in season
Schedule: Open daily, dawn to dusk
Maps: www.parks.ny.gov/documents/parks/ChimneyBluffsTrailMap.pdf
Water availability: Restrooms at parking lot
Trail contact: Chimney Bluffs State Park, 7700 Garner Rd., Wolcott, NY 14590; (315) 947-5205; www.nysparks.state.ny.us/parks/info.asp?parkID=168

Special considerations: Bluff Trail is on the edge of a high bluff with no railings. This hike is not recommended for young children.
Finding the trailhead: From North Syracuse take I-481 North 20.3 miles to NY 3 West. Continue on NY 3 West 8.3 miles and turn left onto NY 104 West. Take NY 104 West 14.2 miles to CR 163 and turn right. Continue on CR 163 2.5 miles to CR 143 (Ridge Road) in Wolcott, and turn right. Turn right again on CR 150, and continue north to Slaght Road. Turn left and drive on Slaght to East Bay Road, and turn right. Continue 0.2 mile to the park entrance on Garner Road. The trail starts on a paved path from the parking lot. GPS: N43 16.871' / W76 55.345'

The Hike

If you doubt the greatness of the Great Lakes, Chimney Bluffs is the place for a change of mind and heart. Here

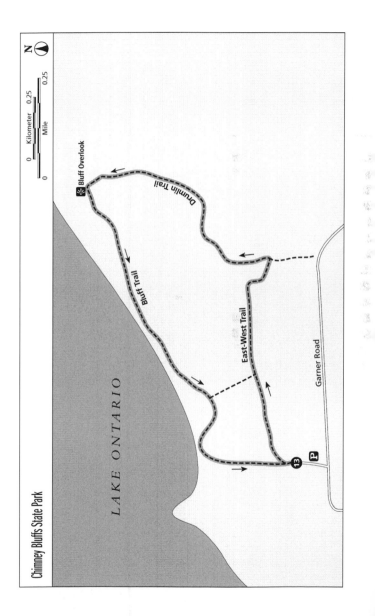

Chimney Bluffs State Park

LAKE ONTARIO

Bluff Overlook

Bluff Trail

Drumlin Trail

East-West Trail

Garner Road

13

P

N

0   Kilometer   0.25

0   0.25
         Mile

Lake Ontario matches its big brother, Lake Superior, in magnificent scenery sculpted by the sheer force of the lake's impact paired with the power of northeastern weather and the dramatic changes that come with the seasons. High waves crash against these clay spires when the gales of December through March turn their attention southward, stealing away the surfaces of these finlike spires and suffering only the most stubborn granules to remain.

Not so long ago, visitors could walk out along the tops of the chimneys—but those days have passed with the winter storms. Hikers are now confined to a narrow cliff edge from which we gain spectacular views of Chimney Bluffs and Lake Ontario's expanse. Deceptively calm from this height of 360 feet above lake level, the lake glistens serenely beneath the summer sunset, belying the tempest that created the rosy spires before you. The far horizon looks strangely solid, but the northern shore in Canada is 53 miles distant—too far to see, even from this height.

The trail leads down a shrub-lined path into a conifer forest, where low spots can be discouragingly muddy even in late spring. As the path emerges from the woods at the edge of the bluff, the Chimneys come into view. Watch out for the cliff edge—there's no railing here or anywhere along the Bluff Trail. Turn left to continue the loop along the cliff (there's a stairway down to another parking area to the right, if you've suddenly discovered a fear of ledges), which descends very gradually to the shoreline. The pebble beach at the end of the Bluff Trail may not look inviting at first glance, but it's a great place to stand to view the Chimney Bluffs from lake level as sunset turns them russet and golden.

Miles and Directions

0.0 Start at the parking lot and walk up the paved path until you see a mowed swath through the grasses to your right. Turn down this path and begin to cross the field of shrubs. You're on the park's East-West Trail.

0.6 Two trails converge here: The East-West Trail continues straight, while the Drumlin Trail goes left and right. Turn left onto the Drumlin Trail. Begin to pass through a conifer forest, with thick grapevines hanging from many of the trees.

1.1 Emerge from the woods at the Bluff Overlook. The Chimneys are to your left. Turn left and continue on the Bluff Trail. As you walk you'll notice that some parts of the trail have crumbled with erosion. In most cases visitors have worn new paths as alternatives to those that have fallen away. Watch your step on this trail, and stop walking when you want to admire the scenery.

1.7 A trail leads left, back into the woods. This is one of several connecting trails that take you back to the developed areas of the park and the parking lot. Turn left here to shorten your hike or continue straight for more of the Bluff Trail.

1.9 When you come out of the woods, you're at lake level at a pebble beach. (FYI: Stop here to stand on the beach and look back at the bluffs before departing.) Turn left and walk across the mowed grass to the paved path that leads to the parking area.

2.2 Arrive back at the parking lot and your vehicle.

14 Labrador Hollow State Unique Area

Stroll the boardwalk for a triple delight: forest-covered hills, bird-filled wetlands, and a sparkling glacial kettle pond.

Distance: 0.5-mile lollipop
Approximate hiking time: 30 minutes
Difficulty: Easy
Trail surface: Sturdy boardwalk
Best season: Year-round
Other trail users: None
Canine compatibility: Leashed dogs permitted
Fees and permits: No fees or permits required
Schedule: Open daily, dawn to dusk
Maps: https://www.dec.ny.gov/docs/regions_pdf/labhollowgeo.pdf

Water availability: None
Trail contact: NYSDEC Region 7 Division of Lands and Forests, 1285 Fisher Ave., Cortland, NY 13045; (607) 753-3095; www.dec.ny.gov/lands/37070.htm
Finding the trailhead: From Syracuse take I-81 South about 18 miles to Tully (exit 14). From Tully take NY 80 East 9.8 miles to NY 91 South. Watch for the sign on the right side of NY 91 for Labrador Hollow and the parking area. The boardwalk begins at the parking area. GPS: N42 47.560' / W76 03.143'

The Hike

How does a natural space qualify for the title of Unique Area? Not surprisingly, the qualifications are different for each property—that, after all, is what makes them unique. In the case of Labrador Hollow, the confluence of several kinds of topography—a narrow, glacially carved valley; surrounding hills several hundred feet high; a pine and hemlock swamp; and marshlands that provide a graceful transition to the open water of a glacial kettle pond—make this area unusually

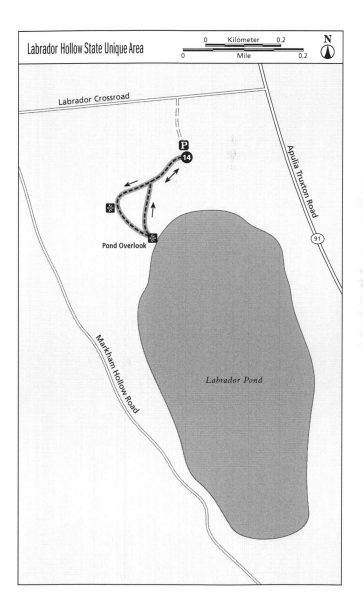

Labrador Hollow State Unique Area

Labrador Crossroad

Apulia Truxton Road

91

Markham Hollow Road

P

14

Pond Overlook

Labrador Pond

N

0   Kilometer   0.2
0   Mile   0.2

special. The Department of Environmental Conservation has made it easy for us to enjoy Labrador Hollow's scenic riches with the installation of a beautiful boardwalk system that brings visitors directly to quality viewpoints.

The 0.5-mile boardwalk leads through several different ecological zones, and the astute observer will see and hear the clues that separate one habitat from another. Wood thrushes and house wrens call in the wooded areas on dry land, while common yellowthroat and willow flycatcher songs dominate the wetlands. Spring peeper calls echo in the marshes, while the rubber-band call of the green frog becomes clearer as the boardwalk approaches the pond. Fiddlehead ferns and pink trilliums gain footholds in the drier area at the beginning of the walk, giving way in the wetland to lily pads and periphyton—a moisture-holding algae that delivers nutrition to plants in dry seasons.

Your walk may be brief, but you'll find plenty to see and hear in this singular environment.

Miles and Directions

0.0 Start at the parking area. Turn right as the loop begins. Pass through woods of mixed evergreens and leafy trees, where trillium and mayapple bloom in spring. Look out from the boardwalk to see the forested hills that define this valley—a stunning sight in autumn.

0.2 A built-in bench provides a great place to stop and admire the view of the hills. Continue around the loop and pass into a swampier area with fewer trees. Don't miss the dead, hollowed tree to your left, with its crazy assortment of woodpecker holes.

0.3 An area with open water appears to your right. Lily pads cover part of the pond, but you might still glimpse a swimming muskrat just below the surface. Look for ducks, geese, herons, and other water-loving birds, and listen for common yellowthroat, marsh wren, song and swamp sparrows, and many different frogs. In a moment you'll reach an excellent overlook for Labrador Pond, a glacial kettle pond. This pond came to be when a calving glacier dropped a huge block of ice in this spot, creating a cavity that filled with water when the ice block melted. Today this pond is a favorite with local canoeists.

0.4 Turn right at the intersection to return to the parking area.

0.5 Complete the loop and return to your vehicle.

15 **Highland Forest County Park**

Here's a forest sampler: A 2.2-mile loop through hardwood and evergreen woodlands to discover one of the area's most popular wilderness parklands.

Distance: 2.2-mile figure-8 loop
Approximate hiking time: 1.25 hours
Difficulty: Moderate
Trail surface: Dirt path
Best season: Year-round
Other trail users: None on hiking trails; different trails for cyclists and skiers
Canine compatibility: Leashed dogs permitted on hiking trails only
Fees and permits: Fee per person for hiking and snowshoeing, day pass required for cross-country skiing
Schedule: Open daily, 8:30 a.m. to 4:30 p.m. Dec through Mar and dawn to dusk Apr through Nov

Maps: www.onondagacounty parks.com/assets/Uploads /HF2016TrailMaps2.pdf
Water availability: At Skyline Lodge and at restrooms near Kernen Shelter
Trail contact: Highland Forest Park, 1254 Highland Park Rd., Fabius, NY 13063; (315) 683-5550; https://www.onondaga countyparks.com/parks /highland-forest
Finding the trailhead: From Syracuse take I-81 South about 18 miles to Tully (exit 14). Drive 11 miles east on NY 80 to Highland Park Road and the entrance to the park. The trails begin at Skyland Lodge. GPS: N42 50.244' / W75 55.385'

The Hike

The oldest and most established of Onondaga County's parks, Highland Forest could serve as a model for parks on the national level. Its scrupulous organization of separate trails for foot traffic and bikes or skis, its clear trail markings

Highland Forest County Park

N

0   Kilometer   0.25

0   Mile   0.25

80

Highland Park Road

Skyline Lodge

P 15

Kernen Junction Trail

Limestone Trail

Kernen Shelter

P

Torbert Shelter

Nature Trail

Bike Trails

Highland Park Road

that leave no room for confusion, and its meticulous maintenance of the trails all make this a world-class park. It's no wonder that everyone we consulted in the Syracuse area recommended that we include Highland Forest in this guide.

Trails in this park range from 0.5-mile wanders to a loop of nearly 9 miles. The North County National Scenic Trail—piggybacking here on the Onondaga Trail of the Finger Lakes Trail System—passes through the park as well. The shorter loop we've chosen allows you to get a sense of what this forest is about on a relatively easy trek, perhaps enticing you to make a longer trip on your next visit.

Begin at the Skyline Lodge by registering in the book at the front desk. With a park of this size—2,759 acres—it's important to let park management know where you're planning to be, so list the trails you plan to hike (Kernen Junction, Nature, and Limestone Trails) in the space provided. Pick up the brochure for the self-guided Nature Trail, which describes the stops in detail.

If you're hiking or cross-country skiing here in winter, the Skyline Lodge Cafe offers a selection of soups and sandwiches from 11 a.m. to 3 p.m., all catered by Bull & Bear Roadhouse in a dining room with a magnificent view. You can rent snowshoes here as well.

Over the creek and through the woods—you'll be glad you spent a day hiking in this wonderfully natural, unusually user-friendly park.

Miles and Directions

0.0 Start at Skyline Lodge and proceed to the well-marked trail gateway signs. Take the trail marked hiking/snowshoeing, and follow the maroon signs for the Kernen Junction Trail.

0.2 Turn left at the trail junction, following the Kernen Junction Trail.

0.3 Cross a dirt road and continue straight. The Finger Lakes and North Country National Scenic Trails join the trail here.

0.5 Turn right onto the Kernen Junction Trail. (The Limestone and Crossover Trails also go straight here.) Cross the road ahead and continue straight.

0.6 The Kernen Shelter is to the right, and a parking lot appears on your left. There are restrooms here. Continue to the trailhead for the Nature Trail (green signs), where you see a wooden board with a clock, thermometer, and trail map. Begin the Nature Trail by walking down five steps to a bridge over the creek.

0.8 Cross two bridges over small streams.

0.9 Reach a junction at a larger bridge. The bike trails go left. Go right over the bridge, briefly sharing the trail with the bicycle/skiing routes. As you step off the bridge, turn immediately left to continue on the Nature Trail. Enter a particularly lovely evergreen forest in which the trees continue to grow at the top while they lose needles and branches below.

1.0 Cross another bridge and turn left at the trail junction. You are leaving the Crossover Trail (gold signs) and the Main Trail (orange signs) and walking exclusively on the Nature Trail.

1.1 Cross the bike trails and continue straight. At the turn go left on the Nature Trail.

1.3 Turn left onto the wide path toward the park office. Bear right ahead as you approach Torbert Shelter. Cross the parking lot to the left and pick up the trail at the information center kiosk on the southeast end of the parking lot, directly to your left. Turn right at the board with the clock and thermometer (do not take the Nature Trail). Follow the Kernen Junction Trail across the road.

1.7 You've retraced your steps along the connecting portion of the Kernen Junction Trail; now bear right onto the Limestone

Trail (pink signs). Cross a mowed area to the hiking/snow-shoeing trail sign. Pass under the sign and begin the Limestone Trail. Through the next several trail junctions, continue straight on the Limestone Trail.

2.0 Walk up a set of steps defined by logs.

2.2 Emerge from the woods onto the mowed yard of Skyline Lodge. Stop at the lodge to record your trail completion time in the register before returning to your vehicle.

16 Bear Swamp State Forest

You can lose the blues in this sun-dappled woodland, but you won't get lost on these well-marked trails through marshy bottomland and drier hardwood forest.

Distance: 3.0-mile loop

Approximate hiking time: 1.5 hours

Difficulty: Moderate

Trail surface: Dirt path

Best season: Year-round

Other trail users: Cross-country skiers, snowmobilers, trail runners, horseback riders

Canine compatibility: Leashed dogs permitted

Fees and permits: No fees or permits required

Schedule: Open daily, dawn to dusk

Maps: www.dec.ny.gov/docs /regions_pdf/bearswampmap 2021.pdf

Water availability: None

Trail contact: New York State Department of Environmental Conservation, Region 7 Lands and Forests, 1285 Fisher Ave., Cortland, NY 13045; (607) 753-3095; www.dec.ny.gov/lands /34420.html

Finding the trailhead: From Syracuse take I-81 South about 22 miles to NY 281 (exit 13). Turn right onto NY 281 and continue 4.4 miles to Cold Brook Road; turn right. Drive to Long Road and turn left. Continue as Long Road becomes Glen Haven Road and then Grinnell Road. Turn right onto West Scott Road and continue 1.3 miles to Bear Swamp Road; keep right on Bear Swamp Road. In 2.1 miles turn left onto Hartnett Road. Park along the roadside near the trailhead for Trail 1. Look for a wooden display sign with a narrow trail running into the woods. GPS: N42 44.929' / W76 18.980'

Bear Swamp State Forest

N

Kilometer
0   0.3

0   0.3
Mile

Guidepost #4

Snowshoe Trail

Trail 4 Begins

Hartnett Road

Trail 5 Begins

Guidepost #3

Guidepost #2

Corduroy
Bridge

Trail 1 Begins

P 16

41

The Hike

Bear Swamp is a testament to reforestation as a viable way to reclaim clear-cut fields and turn them back into lush woodland. It's hard to imagine today that these 3,316 acres were used as farmland as recently as the 1930s, before the Great Depression drove many farmers to seek more lucrative employment.

When the farmers abandoned this land, New York State bought it up quickly, working with the Civilian Conservation Corps to plant Norway spruce, red and white pine, and larch. Other hardwoods migrated here on their own, especially the maple trees that cover so much northeastern land. In fall this forest fills with fiery shades of ruby, topaz, and gold when the leafy trees celebrate the change of seasons.

While its trails were constructed with cross-country skiing in mind, Bear Swamp offers an equally high-quality experience in spring, summer, and fall for hikers who can enjoy the well-established, clearly marked trails. Thirteen miles of trails provide many choices for hikers. We've chosen a loop that provides fairly easy walking through areas of managed forest and young hardwoods, moving from groves of pine and spruce to ash, cherry, and maple. This healthy forest enjoys responsible management, making this trail particularly appealing at any time of year.

Miles and Directions

0.0 From Hartnett Road, you will see two paths: a wide path with a kiosk that bears a marker that says cy 44 and a narrow path to the left with a round orange marker that says TRAIL 1 in white print. Take the narrower path with the Trail 1 marker (the wider trail is for snowmobiles). In spring note the mounds of vinca (periwinkle) blooming at the trailhead. Trail 1 goes straight and to the left; turn left.

0.2 Cross a gravel-covered corduroy bridge over a small stream.

0.4 A drainage pipe forms a bridge over a small, slowly moving stream. Continue straight.

0.6 Come to a brown sign with a yellow "2" on it. This is Guide-post 2, part of the orientation system installed by the DEC. You've reached an old fire road, left over from the 1930s when fire lanes helped provide access to young conifer plantations. The surrounding red oak and red pine were planted during that time. Continue straight ahead.

0.8 At the intersection turn right and follow the Trail 1 signs.

1.0 Reach Guidepost 3. Turn right and continue to follow Trail 1. As you walk you may notice the difference between the forests on your right and left. The forest on your right has been thinned to allow new, young trees to germinate; the left-hand forest remains in its natural state.

1.4 At Guidepost 4, Snowshoe Trail to the right leads back to Hartnett Road. (Option: If you'd like a quick way back to your car at this point, this is an easy exit route.) Continue straight.

2.2 Come to Hartnett Road. From here the hike is a little more difficult, with some hilly terrain. (Option: To end your hike here, turn right and walk up the road to your car.) Cross the road and reenter the woods a little to the right, where you see an orange marker for Trail 4. Again, the ground around the entrance to the trail is covered in vinca.

2.3 A spur trail goes to the right. Continue left.

2.4 Cross a culvert over a stream and begin a steady incline to a barrier made of five large boulders, placed to keep motorized vehicles off the trail. Continue straight. A trail goes off to the left; pass it and take the next right.

2.5 A road goes left and right here. Cross and continue straight. At this point you're following the markers for Trail 5.

2.6 Here the trail goes left and right. Turn right and start down the hill. In a moment turn left to continue on Trail 5.

2.8 Take the trail to the left. Hartnett Road is now straight ahead.

2.9 Reach Hartnett Road again. Turn left and walk on the road to return to your car.

3.0 Complete the loop at your vehicle.

17 High Vista Preserve

A forest floor covered with wildflowers in late spring and summer, a small creek tributary meandering through a young forest . . . this peaceful woodland is a well-kept secret.

Distance: 1.8-mile lollipop
Approximate hiking time: 45 minutes
Difficulty: Easy
Trail surface: Dirt path
Best season: Apr through Nov
Other trail users: Hikers only
Canine compatibility: Leashed dogs permitted
Fees and permits: No fees or permits required
Schedule: Open daily, dawn to dusk, Apr through Nov; road to preserve not plowed Dec 1 to Apr 1
Maps: www.fllt.org/wp-content /uploads/2014/12/High-Vista .pdf
Water availability: None

Trail contact: Finger Lakes Land Trust, 202 East Court St., Ithaca, NY 14850; (607) 275-9487; www.fllt.org
Special considerations: Creek crossings may be difficult in early spring and after heavy rain (no bridges).
Finding the trailhead: From NY 41 south of Skaneateles, turn onto Vincent Hill Road West, just north of the Cortland/Onondaga County line. Drive about 0.3 mile to a small parking area on the right side of the road. The trail begins across the road, about 0.2 mile from the parking area. GPS: N42 46.230' / W76 15.655'

The Hike

Once upon a time, these 120 acres lay open and denuded on this sunny hillside, but those days are long gone. And while this little preserve retains the word "vista" in its name, the only view here peers deeper into the fairly young woods that now cover the terrain. The Finger Lakes Land Trust acquired this property back in 1993, and the organization now maintains the trail and looks after the woods, wetland, and ravine that grace the land.

The simple loop hike wanders first through an old orchard, followed by young hardwoods and hemlocks. The trail crosses a number of small streams and the larger Fair Haven Creek and wanders past clusters of wildflowers in spring, from violets and trillium to wild strawberry and jack-in-the-pulpit. Many fern species fill the gaps between wildflowers, creating a sheltering understory for ground-feeding birds, chipmunks, squirrels, and other small animals.

The real treat here is the opportunity to spot cerulean warblers, which nest in the preserve, and many other warblers from late April through May. As in any hardwood forest, woodpeckers can be heard hammering in the trees—watch for northern flicker and downy, hairy, and red-bellied woodpeckers.

As for that high vista . . . if you hike here in late fall or early spring, when the trees are without leaves, you can glimpse the southern end of Skaneateles Lake from the highest points on the trail.

Miles and Directions

0.0 Start from the parking area and walk up the road to the trailhead. This is also the parking area for the adjacent Hinchcliff Family Preserve, so be sure to walk southwest up the road to High Vista, rather than taking the Hinchcliff trailhead to the north.

0.2 The trail begins here to your left; enter the preserve and follow the blue blazes.

0.5 The intersection is the beginning of the loop. Take the left branch.

0.7 Cross Fair Haven Creek on big, flat rocks. This may be tricky in spring when the creek rises with snowmelt.

1.0 Cross Fair Haven Creek again. You may need to hunt for the best place to cross, particularly in spring. There are several spots with large rocks that are close enough together to provide solid footing.

1.1 Reach the junction with the yellow trail to the left. (This trail leads out to Vincent Hill Road.) Bear right on the blue trail.

1.3 Complete the loop. Turn left and follow the trail back out to your vehicle.

1.8 Arrive back at the parking area.

18 Fillmore Glen State Park

One waterfall after another tumbles through a narrow, lushly forested gorge, making this a delicious hike on a hot summer day.

Distance: 2.4-mile loop
Approximate hiking time: 1.5 hours
Difficulty: Moderate
Trail surface: Dirt path, some stone stairs
Best season: June through Oct
Other trail users: None
Canine compatibility: Leashed dogs permitted
Fees and permits: Entry fee per vehicle in season
Schedule: Open daily dawn to dusk; check the park website for specific trail opening dates
Maps: www.parks.ny.gov/docu ments/parks/FillmoreGlenTrail Map.pdf
Water availability: Restrooms at main pavilion and in campground

Trail contact: Fillmore Glen State Park, 1686 NY 38, Moravia, NY 13118; (315) 497-0130; www .parks.ny.gov/parks/fillmoreglen
Special considerations: Some trails close in seasons with flooding. Call the park to check the trail opening date, especially in May. Watch for fallen, loose shale on the path.
Finding the trailhead: From Syracuse take NY 5 West about 22 miles to the junction with NY 38 in Auburn. Turn south onto NY 38 and continue 17 miles to the park entrance in Moravia. Park at the main pavilion; the trailhead is behind the building and up the paved path. GPS: N42 41.932' / W76 24.981'

The Hike

If you're going to take only one hike recommended in this guide, make it Fillmore Glen. Rarely do we find such a magical combination of striking geological formations, glistening gorge walls that weep with spring runoff, a storybook forest, and no fewer than five waterfalls—including one that plummets from a creek tributary at the top of the gorge. Tie all of this with an ingenious system of eight bridges that cross and recross the gorge, laced together by a pathway reinforced with natural stone guard walls, and you have the kind of hiking experience that makes the Finger Lakes region famous.

It's no surprise that glaciers played the initial role in shaping the gorge as the rush of glacial meltwater tore through the area and slashed through the surface shale to the limestone bedrock below. Today the surrounding shale continues to erode—you're likely to see recent crumbles as you hike—but the tenacious vegetation plays a role in holding much of it in place, covering the jagged rock faces with mosses, lichens, and vines.

While this hike is fairly easy in dry weather, the gorge creates a microclimate in which the humidity remains high. Stone steps and earthen pathways can be slippery, and water often drips (or cascades) from the porous shale walls, especially after a heavy rain. Two words to the wise on this:

(1) Wear footwear that will grip in wet situations.

(2) Don't miss the hanging gardens of ferns and clinging vines that result from the constant seeps through the multi-layered shale.

Chances are, you don't often think about the thirteenth president of the United States, so it may not occur to you that this park is actually named for him. Millard Fillmore was born in this area, just outside Moravia, and the park contains a replica of the cabin in which he was born. You'll find it as you proceed to the main pavilion to begin your hike; it's on the south side of the parking area.

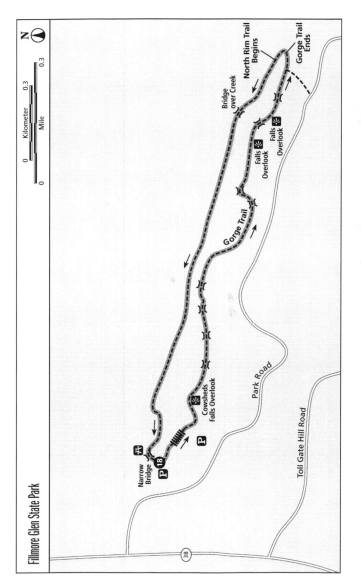

Fillmore Glen State Park

N

Kilometer 0.3

Mile 0.3

North Rim Trail Begins

Gorge Trail Ends

Bridge over Creek

Falls Overlook

Falls Overlook

Gorge Trail

Cowsheds Falls Overlook

Park Road

Narrow Bridge

P 18

P

Toll Gate Hill Road

38

Miles and Directions

0.0   Start at the trailhead behind the pavilion and up the paved path.

0.1   The swimming area is to the left of the path, created by one of two dams in Dry Creek. Keep right and continue on the paved path.

0.2   Turn right onto the Gorge Trail. (Don't cross the bridge here; that's the route to the North Rim.) Take the stairway to the right; it's 140 steps to the top. (Option: Park in the lot at the top of the stairs to save yourself the fairly aerobic climb.) At the top of the steps turn left on the Gorge Trail.

0.3   Reach the overlook for Cowsheds Falls. Turn right and continue to the first of eight bridges on the Gorge Trail.

0.4   Cross Bridge 1 and enter the dense, sultry forest. Stop here a moment to notice the fascinating patterns of moss on the trees and the change in the light quality as the sun works to filter through the leafy canopy. On the other side of this patch of forest, cross Bridge 2.

0.5   Cross Bridge 3.

0.6   Cross Bridge 4 and begin a steady incline.

0.7   Reach the top of the incline and a small waterfall.

0.8   Cross a series of platforms over runoff streams.

0.9   Cross Bridges 5 and 6.

1.0   A tributary creek originating at the top of the gorge sends a spectacular waterfall down through the glen wall. As you continue on the trail, don't miss the hanging gardens created by the seeps through the stacked shale walls.

1.1   Cross Bridge 7 and go up a staircase of about thirty steps.

1.2   Walk down sixteen steps to a falls overlook. When you're ready, walk up sixteen steps on the other side of the overlook and continue on the trail.

1.3   Come to Bridge 8, the last bridge on the Gorge Trail. The South Rim Trail crosses the bridge. To complete the Gorge Trail, do not cross this bridge—continue straight. To follow the North Rim Trail to make a loop, as described here, continue straight as well. In about 200 feet the Gorge Trail ends. (Option: Return to the trailhead by retracing your steps on the Gorge Trail.) To continue the loop, climb to the North Rim using the switchbacks ahead. (FYI: The climb to the North Rim involves a 150-foot elevation change.)

1.4   At the top of the gorge turn left on the North Rim Trail. Cross a board over a feeder stream.

1.7   Reach the source of the large waterfall you saw in the gorge. Cross a bridge over this tributary creek.

2.3   After a gentle descent on stone steps, bear left on the fork in the trail and proceed down a series of steps defined by railroad ties, followed by more stone steps. At the bottom you've reached Dry Creek and the picnic area on the north side of the gorge. Bear right and cross the parking lot to your left.

2.4   Cross the creek using the narrow bridge over the spillway, and arrive back at your vehicle in the parking lot.

Clubs and Trail Groups

Adirondack Mountain Club, Onondaga Chapter; www
.adk-on.org. The club offers a variety of hikes and programs
to share the joy and knowledge of outdoor recreation.

Syracuse Area Outdoor Adventure Club, www.meetup
.com/adventurers-103. For people who want to get outside,
have fun, and meet others with similar interests, the group
holds regularly scheduled hikes and seasonal adventures.

Onondaga Audubon Society, https://www.onondaga
audubon.com. The Audubon society promotes a greater
appreciation of wildlife, land, water, and other natural
resources through field trips, sanctuary management, and
environmental education.

Syracuse University Outing Club, https://suoc.syr.edu.
Students of Syracuse University and the SUNY College of
Environmental Science and Forestry join to promote the
enjoyment of the national environment with many trips and
outings.

Finger Lakes Land Trust, 202 East Court St., Ithaca 14850;
(607) 275-9487; www.fllt.org. This nonprofit land trust
works to preserve lands that define the character of the Finger Lakes region.

Day Hiker Checklist

- ❏ camera
- ❏ compass/GPS unit
- ❏ daypack
- ❏ first-aid kit
- ❏ fleece jacket
- ❏ food
- ❏ guidebook
- ❏ headlamp/flashlight with extra batteries and bulbs
- ❏ hat
- ❏ insect repellent
- ❏ knife/multipurpose tool
- ❏ map
- ❏ matches in waterproof container and fire starter
- ❏ mobile phone
- ❏ rain gear
- ❏ step-counting device (smartphone, watch)
- ❏ sunglasses
- ❏ sunscreen
- ❏ watch
- ❏ water
- ❏ water bottles/water hydration system

About the Author

Randi Minetor has written more than fifty books to date for imprints of Rowman & Littlefield, including three editions of *Hiking Waterfalls New York*, *Hiking Through History New York*, *Hiking the Lower Hudson River Valley*, *Hiking the Catskills* with co-author Stacey Freed, and *Best Easy Day Hikes* guides to Rochester, Buffalo, Syracuse, Albany, and the Hudson River Valley. She is also the author of *Birding New England*, *Birding Florida*, and *Birding Texas* for FalconGuides, *New York Off the Beaten Path* (10th edition) for Globe Pequot, and she has written seven books in the nonfiction *Death in the National Parks* series for Lyons Press. She and her husband, photographer Nic Minetor, live in Rochester.